HIGHER EDUCATION INTERLIBRARY LOAN MANAGEMENT BENCHMARKS

The Questionnaire for this report was designed by Elaine Sanchez, Texas State University, San Marco

D1529785

ISBN: 1-57440-112-2   ©2009 Primary Research Group Inc.

Table of Contents

List of Participants

Acadia University
Alamo Community College
Allan Hancock College
Assiniboine Community College
Athabasca University
Binghamton University (SUNY)
Bluffton University
Bridgewater College
Burlington County College Library
Butler University
Coastal Carolina University
College of DuPage
College of St. Catherine
Columbus State University
Community College of Rhode Island
Connecticut College
Connors State College
Dickinson College
Eastern Washington University
Elon University
Fairleigh Dickinson University
Felician College
Gannon University
Georgian Court University
Gogebic Community College
Grant MacEwan College Library
Harding University
Holy Family University
Indiana University of PA
Indiana University
Purdue University
Indiana University South Bend
Jackson State Community College
Kansas City Community College
Lamar University
Lehigh Carbon Community College
Louisiana Tech University
Luther College
McDaniel College
McNeese State University
Medicine Hat College
Mercer University, Macon GA
Messiah College
Nazareth College of Rochester

Northeast Iowa Community College
Northern Lights College
Northwestern College of Iowa
Northwestern Connecticut Community
  College
Ohio University
Ottawa University
Ozarks Technical Community College
Pace University
Pennsylvania College of Technology
Pikes Peak Community College
Presbyterian College
Randolph-Macon College
Renton Technical College
Ripon College
Rivier College
Roger Williams University
Royal Military College of Canada
Saint Paul University
San Francisco State University
Santa Rosa Junior College
South University
Texas A&M University - Corpus Christi
The College of St. Scholastica
Three Rivers Community College
Trent University
University of Cincinnati
University of Colorado, Boulder
University of Connecticut School of Law
University of Houston
University of Manitoba, Ft. Garry Campus
University of Maryland Eastern Shore
University of Nebraska at Kearney
University of South Florida St. Petersburg
Utah State University
Vancouver Community College
Virginia Commonwealth University
Virginia Community College System
Western Washington University
Western Washington University
William Paterson University of New Jersey
Wilson College
Wright State University

List of Tables

SUMMARY OF MAIN FINDINGS

Interlibrary Loan Transaction Volume

For the libraries in the sample, interlibrary loan volume has increased significantly over the past three years, by a median aggregate volume of 9.5%. A few libraries experienced extremely rapid aggregate growth so that the mean aggregate (the growth rate of all libraries divided by the number in the sample) rose by a cumulative 21.29% in the three-year period 2005 to 2008. For community and 4-year/M.A. level colleges, the increase was particularly dramatic, 36% for the former and nearly that for the latter. Growth of lending volume (an average of in-bound and out-bound) was much higher in the U.S. than in Canada.

Performance of Interlibrary Loan User Surveys

Close to 15% of the libraries in the sample have performed a user survey of ILL services within the past four years. Research libraries were somewhat more likely than others to have done so.

Turnaround Time for Borrowing Articles & Books

The mean turnaround time for borrowing articles was 4.54 days; it was slightly lower for private than public college libraries, 4.22 days vs. 4.82 days. Canadian libraries took nearly a day longer than U.S.-based libraries. Turnaround time tended to drop as college enrollment increased.

Mean turnaround time for borrowing requests for books was longer, a mean of 7.67 days, 8.7 for public colleges and 6.31 for private colleges. The range of time for book borrowing requests was extraordinary, ranging from a minimum of 1 day to a maximum of 30 days. Community colleges took the longest; those borrowing had to wait a mean of 9.2 days to receive their books from their partners. Requests from Canada took longer to fulfill than requests from the United States, by a considerable margin of more than 1.5 days.

Turnaround Time for Lending Articles & Books

The mean time it took to fulfill a request for lending articles from one's own collection was 1.63 days. The discrepancy between time spent in fulfilling a lending request and time spent in receiving an item requested from another party is likely due to two causes: 1) Time in transit, which is not accounted for in fulfillment of a loan request but is accounted for in borrowing, and 2) the nature of the libraries that responded to the survey. It may be that respondents have a greater interest in interlibrary loan and may have an above-average response time. Public colleges took slightly longer than private colleges to fulfill requests and Canadian colleges took longer than those in the United States.

For book lending requests mean time of fulfillment was 2.29 days but mean fulfillment time was far longer for public than for private colleges, 2.73 vs. 1.63 days. It was particularly high for research universities, averaging 3.3 days.

Turnaround Time for Lending Videos

Mean turnaround time for lending videos was 1.92 days, with Canadians nearly twice as fast as Americans in this respect. Mean borrowing time for videos was 6.89 days, suggesting a long time in transit for videos. It took community colleges in the sample a mean of nearly 9 days to receive a video via interlibrary loan. Mean borrowing time for Canadians was 9.75 days.

Mean Spending for Shipping & Courier Fees

Mean spending for the libraries in the sample on shipping & courier fees related to interlibrary loan was $6,857, with a median of just $2,042. The research universities in the sample spent a mean of more than $20,000. As might be expected, spending rose with enrollment size. Colleges with fewer than 2,000 students FTE spent a mean of $2,079.89, while those with more than 15,000 students spent a mean of $14,843.36.

Policies on the Interlibrary Loan of Textbooks

Close to 66% of the libraries in the sample allow interlibrary loan of college textbooks. Only 41.2% allow the interlibrary loan of state-adopted college textbooks. Only 27.27% of community colleges allowed the interlibrary loan of state-adopted college textbooks, while 55.56% of research universities did so. Many libraries said that they treated textbooks as they would any other book for library loan periods; some libraries had a policy of not buying textbooks.

Ebook Licenses & Interlibrary Loan

5.13% of the libraries in the sample say that their ebook licenses allow for some form of interlibrary loan. Private colleges that offer B.A./M.A. degrees were the most likely to have negotiated this privilege with ebook vendors. All were U.S.-based institutions.

Interlibrary Loan with Foreign Countries

Two-thirds of the libraries in the sample do interlibrary loan with libraries in foreign countries. The more complex the degree offered by the college, the more likely the library was to engage in interlibrary loan with foreign countries; 44.45% of community college libraries do interlibrary loan with foreign countries, while close to 89% of research libraries do so.

Percentage of Colleges in a State or Provincial Borrowing Network

86.75% of the colleges in the sample have a state or provincial borrowing network in their state. Close to 77% of the libraries in the sample participate in a state or provincial borrowing network.

More than 86% of private colleges in the sample participate in a state borrowing network, while 71.7% of public college libraries participate in one. B.A./M.A. level colleges were the most likely to participate in a state borrowing network; more than 94% of those in the sample do so.

Use of State ILL/DD/EDD Statistics

A shade more than half of the libraries in the sample use state ILL/DD/EDD statistics for any reason. Private colleges and research universities were the most likely to use the statistics.

Percentage of Libraries in a State Network that Identify Net Lender and Performs Load Leveling

A shade more than 43% of the colleges in the sample are in state networks that identify net lenders and perform load leveling.

Use of Fax Delivery

73% of the libraries in the sample use fax delivery for interlibrary loan fulfillment. Public libraries were far more likely than private libraries to use fax as a means of fulfillment; more than 83% of public libraries faxed documents to satisfy interlibrary loan requests, while only a shade less than 55% of private college libraries did so. More than 95% of community colleges used fax delivery in interlibrary loan.

Use of Email Attachment Delivery

Close to 72% of the libraries in the sample use email attachments as a means to deliver documents in interlibrary loan; close to 79% photocopy documents to satisfy interlibrary loan requests. More than 86% of community colleges send photocopies to satisfy some interlibrary loans. All of the Canadian libraries in the sample use photocopies to satisfy some interlibrary loan requests.

Use of the Actual Document in Interlibrary Loan

About 55.3% of the libraries in the sample use the actual document to satisfy interlibrary loan requests. All Canadian libraries in the sample used the actual documents, while slightly less than half of U.S. libraries did so. 74.12% of the libraries in the sample use scanned documents to satisfy interlibrary loan requests, while 29.41% use e-text from databases to satisfy loan requests. More than 45% of Canadian colleges in the sample used e-text, as did nearly 39% of the research universities in the sample. Only 6.25% of colleges with fewer than 2,000 students used e-text in interlibrary loan requests.

Participation in Distance Learning Programs

34.12% of the libraries in the sample have facilities or personnel specifically assigned to service a distance education program.

Use of Interlibrary Loan for Intra-College Materials Transfers

A shade more than 47% of the libraries in the sample use their interlibrary loan facilities to facilitate loans of materials between campuses or units of their own institution. Community colleges and larger colleges in terms of overall enrollment were the most likely to use their interlibrary loan facilities in this way.

Percentage of Libraries that Charge a Fee for Interlibrary Loan

Only 14.12% of the libraries in the sample charge a fee for interlibrary loan. More than 22% of research universities charged a fee.

Trends in the Use of Fax Delivery

Use of fax delivery has significantly declined. More than 53% of the libraries in the sample say that their use of fax delivery in interlibrary loan has decreased while only 11.69% say that it has increased. Public colleges, especially community colleges, accounted for virtually all colleges that had increased the use of fax in interlibrary loan. Decreased use was most marked by research universities, 80% of whom had decreased use of fax in interlibrary loan. All libraries that had increased use of fax were U.S.-based.

Trends in the Use of Email Attachments

For nearly two-thirds of the libraries in the sample, use of email attachments in interlibrary loan has increased, and it decreased for only 2.63%. 80% of private college libraries have had an increase in the use of email attachments in interlibrary loan; it has particularly increased for private, 4-year colleges.

Trends in the Use of Photocopies

For more than 57% of the libraries in the sample, use of photocopies in interlibrary loan had decreased and had increased for only 9.1%.

Trends in the Use of the Actual Document

For 35.7% of the libraries in the sample, the use of the actual document in interlibrary loan has remained the same, while for 17.14% it has increased and for 22.86% it has decreased. For private college libraries, the use of the actual document has increased more than it has decreased, while the reverse is true of the public college libraries. Libraries that offer less complex degrees were more likely than others to have increased the use of the actual document in interlibrary loan.

Trends in the Use of Scanned Documents

The use of scanned documents in interlibrary loan has increased dramatically. For more than 70% of the libraries in the sample, use of scanned documents in interlibrary loan has increased, while it had decreased for none. For the research libraries in the sample, nearly 87% had increased use of scanning in interlibrary loan.

Trends in the Use of E-text from Databases

The use of e-text from databases has also increased significantly, increasing for 35.3% of the libraries in the sample and decreasing for only 1.47%. The larger the college in terms of FTE enrollment, the greater the percentage of college libraries that had increased their use of e-text from databases in interlibrary loan.

Trends in the Use of Interlibrary Loan for Intra-Campus Transfers

For 28.57% of the libraries in the sample, the use of the college's interlibrary loan facilities for transfers of materials between different campuses or units of the same college has increased, while it has decreased for only 7.14% of the libraries in the sample. Public college libraries and community colleges were particularly likely to experience an increase in the use of interlibrary loan facilities for inter-campus transfers of materials.

Trends in Fees for Interlibrary Loan

For 5.88% of libraries in the sample, fees for use of interlibrary loan have increased but have decreased for 7.35%.

Nearly two-thirds of the libraries in the sample have ever shared full text articles from their subscribed databases.

Views of Librarians on the Extent and Manner in Which Licensing Agreements Should be Documented and Followed

70.67% of the libraries in the sample believe that licensing agreements with publishers and other vendors must be documented and followed; 26.67% mostly agree with this, and 2.67% mostly disagree. None strongly disagree. Close to 81% of private colleges strongly agree that licensing agreements must be documented and followed, while 65.31% of public colleges believe the same.

12.16% of librarians in the sample strongly agree that it is acceptable policy to share fulltext database articles without having to verify publisher approval in every case, while 31.1% mostly agree with this and the same percentage mostly disagree. 25.68% strongly disagree with this policy. U.S. libraries were more likely to agree with this policy than were Canadian libraries.

Views on the Role of the ILL Staff in Licensing

29.17% of the libraries in the sample strongly agree with the statement that interlibrary loan staff should have the individual in charge of database licenses also verify license issues.

22.54% of survey participants strongly agree that the ILL staff should have direct access to the library's ERMS (electronic resource management system) to review licenses; another 22.54% mostly agree with this position. However, more than a third strongly disagreed and 21.13% mostly disagreed. At 4-year/M.A. level institutions, more than 57% strongly disagreed with this position.

Close to 13% of the libraries surveyed strongly agreed that license issue questions relating to interlibrary loan at their institution are handled on an ad hoc, as-needed basis, without a written set or practices; close to 43% mostly agreed with this statement. A bit more than 44% disagreed, nearly split between those that strongly disagreed and mostly disagreed.

Role of the Acquisitions Staff in Maintaining Licensing Agreements

About 64% of the libraries in the sample strongly or mostly agreed that the Acquisitions staff maintains the licensing agreements for the library.

Number of Separate Library Centers Maintained for Interlibrary Loan

For 91.67% of the libraries in the sample, one unit of the library handled all the interlibrary loan and document delivery functions of the library as a whole. Interestingly, figures for smaller libraries were very similar to those for larger libraries and size was not an important factor in the maintenance of more than one center for interlibrary loan and document delivery.

Departmental Control of the ILL Staff in the Library Organizational Hierarchy

For about 21.2% of the libraries surveyed, the ILL department is under the auspices of the library's reference department. This was so for 31.82% of the community colleges in the sample, and for 36.36% of the Canadian libraries. Only 10% of colleges with more than 15,000 students had the ILL department under the auspices of the reference department.

For 28.24% of the libraries in the sample, the ILL department is under the auspices of the circulation department. This was the arrangement for nearly 41% of the community colleges in the sample and for half of all libraries with fewer than 2,000 enrolled students, full time equivalent.

For 21.2% of libraries surveyed, the ILL department is under the auspices of the access services department. This was the case for nearly 28% of the research universities in the sample and for 24.66% of the American colleges. No Canadian college in the sample had their ILL department under the auspices of the access services department.

For 21.18% of the libraries in the sample, the ILL department is under the auspices of the document delivery services department. Once again only U.S. colleges had such arrangements.

For approximately 13% of the libraries surveyed, the ILL department was under the auspices of the technical services department. This was true for 18.52% of public colleges but only 3.23% of private colleges; it was true for 27.27% of the Canadian colleges in the sample.

For 11.76% of the libraries in the sample, the ILL department is under the auspices of the collection development department, while for 21.18% it was under the control of some other department not previously specified.

For 21.2% of the libraries in the sample, DD/EDD is under the auspices of the reference department; this is the case for more than 24% of public colleges, 16.14% of private colleges, 41% of community colleges and more than 45% of Canadian colleges. For 20% of colleges in the sample it was under the auspices of the circulation department; this was the case for nearly 44% of colleges with fewer than 2,000 students, FTE. For 17.65% of the colleges in the sample, the DD/EDD function is under the auspices of the access services. All were U.S.-based colleges and, in general, the more complex the degree offered, the more likely that the college was to have the DD/EED function under the auspices of the access services department.

For 7.06% of the libraries in the sample the DD/EDD function was under the control of the document delivery department. All with this arrangement were public colleges. For 9.41% of those surveyed, the DD/EDD function was under the auspices of the technical services department. Most with this arrangement were community colleges or 4-year/M.A. degree-granting institutions. For only 1.18% of the colleges in the sample, DD/EDD was controlled by the collection development department. For close to a quarter of libraries surveyed, the DD/EDD function was under the control of a department not previously cited above.

For 67.57% of the libraries in the sample, the circulation department handled "any part" of the ILL/DD or EDD function. For Canadian libraries, this was 90%; 65.1% for U.S.-based libraries in the sample.

Use of Automated ILL Systems

39.76% of the libraries in the sample use OCLC's ILLiad for interlibrary loan. The more complex the degree offered by the college, the more likely it was to use ILLiad. 9.1% of the community colleges in the sample used ILLiad, while 66.67% of the research universities used it. Use was far more pervasive in the U.S. than in Canada; 43.66% of U.S. libraries in the sample used it, while 18.18% of Canadian libraries did so.

37.35% of the libraries surveyed use the OCLC ILL subsystem. 54.55% of community college libraries in the sample used this system. A shade more than a third of the libraries in the sample used the automated system OCLC Odyssey. Half of all research universities in the sample used Odyssey. All Odyssey users were U.S.-based institutions.

55.24% of the libraries in the sample used Ariel; 66.07% of the private college libraries in the sample did so, as did nearly 73% of Canadian college libraries and 80% of libraries of institutions with from 5,000 to 10,000 students, FTE.

10.84% of the libraries in the sample used Docline. Docline was used exclusively by the U.S. colleges in the sample and only by colleges in the sample with more than 2,000 students, FTE.

21.69% of the libraries in the sample used WorldCat Local.

About 23% of the libraries in the sample routinely use link resolvers in interlibrary loan operations.

6.1% of the libraries in the sample use OCLC's E-Serials Holdings. Most users were Ph.D.-level or research universities. More than 45% of Canadian libraries in the sample did so, though, interestingly, research university libraries were no more likely than others to use link resolvers in their interlibrary loan efforts.

Impact of Digital Rights Management Control Technologies on Interlibrary Loan

41.67% of the libraries in the sample say that digital rights management control technologies employed by publishers or hardware manufacturers have affected the ability to utilize electronic articles or e-reserves, digital copying, digital document delivery or interlibrary loan. Public colleges have been more impacted than private colleges, and more than 50% or research and Ph.D.-level universities have had digital rights management control technologies employed by publishers or hardware manufacturers impact the ability to utilize electronic articles or e-reserves, digital copying, digital document delivery or interlibrary loan. More than 70% of the Canadian libraries in the sample say that they have been so impacted. In general, the larger the college in terms of FTE enrollment, the more likely the college was to be impacted by digital rights management control technologies.

Percentage of Libraries that have Tried to Negotiate Broader License Terms for Interlibrary Loan

20% of the libraries in the sample have ever tried to negotiate broader license terms for institutional and patron use of their digital collections, specifically for interlibrary loan and e-reserve use. More than 36% of research universities have tried to do this, as have a quarter of colleges in Canada in the sample.

Trends in What is Reported in ILL Statistics

A shade more than 47% of the libraries in the sample report turnaround time in their ILL statistics. Only 38.7% of private college libraries do so, while close to 52% of public college libraries did. U.S.-based libraries were more likely to report turnaround statistics than were their Canadian counterparts.

43.53% of the libraries in the sample report who borrowed from whom in their ILL statistics. Half of all public colleges included such information, while only 32.26% of private colleges did. More than 59% of community colleges reported such information.

Only 34.12% of the colleges in the sample report the most requested books and journals in their ILL statistics. Close to 39% of public college libraries report these statistics and, in general, the more complex the degree offered by the college, the more likely its library was to report most requested books and journal articles in their ILL statistics. U.S. libraries were more than twice as likely as their Canadian counterparts to report such data.

Close to 85% of the libraries in the sample report number of items lent in their ILL statistics. The more complex the degree offered, the less likely was a college to make such revelations. Data for items borrowed was nearly identical.

74.12% of the libraries in the sample report the number of unfilled requests in their ILL statistics. The larger colleges in terms of FTE enrollment were more likely than the smaller colleges to report the number of unfilled requests.

61.18% of the libraries in the sample report the number of photocopies in their ILL statistics. About 67% report returnables in their ILL statistics. Canadian libraries were more likely than American ones to report returnables.

Close to 52% of the libraries in the sample report non-returnables in their statistics. The more complex the degree offered, the more likely the college was to report returnables.

40% of the libraries in the sample report their in-state loans in their ILL statistics. More than 59% of community colleges did so. 36.47% of libraries reported their out-of-state loans. Only 11.76% reported international loans; more than 36% of Canadian libraries in the sample reported international loans, as did 20% of all colleges with more than 20,000 students, FTE.

18.82% report Ariel delivery in their ILL stats, while 14.12% reported the incidence of email delivery. Incidence of fax delivery was reported by 15.3% of the libraries in the sample, most frequently by research universities. 17.65% reported ILLiad transfers; all were U.S.-based libraries.

11.76% of the libraries in the sample reported frequency of use of U.S. mail in their ILL operations statistics and 8.24% reported on the frequency of use of other carriers.

8.24% of the libraries in the sample report walk-ins in their ILL statistics. Mostly these were Ph.D.-level, but not research universities.

Use of Workflow Studies of the Interlibrary Loan Process

About 22% of the libraries in the sample have performed workflow studies to review practices and staffing in ILL/DD/EDD applications. In general, the more sophisticated the degree offered, the more likely the institution was to have performed workflow studies of this kind. Also, 60% of all Canadian libraries in the sample have performed workflow studies for ILL/DD/EDD applications.

Degrees Held by ILL Staffers

Close to 40% of the libraries in the sample require an MLS or MLIS librarian to supervise the interlibrary loan or document delivery department. More than 58% of private college libraries required a librarian with one of these degrees to supervise the ILL or document delivery departments. Interestingly, only 21.43% of research universities in the sample had such requirements, as did close to 47% of colleges with fewer than 2,000 students enrolled, FTE.

Mean ILL/DD/EDD Staff Size

The staff size (FTE) of the ILL/DD or EDD staff for the libraries in the sample was a mean of 1.9 and a median of 1.13; the range was 0 to 16.25. Staff size rose with the complexity of the degree offered, increasing from a mean of 1.1 for community colleges to 3.33 for research universities. Staff size also rose with college size, increasing from a mean of 1.12 for colleges with fewer than 2,000 students to 2.59 for colleges with more than 15,000 students. The mean number of full-time MLS professionals on the ILL/DD/EDD staff for the libraries in the sample was 0.52, with a maximum of 2. The number of part-time MLS or MLIS professionals on the library's ILL/DD or EDD staff was 0.34.

The mean number of student workers, defined as 10-hour per week allocations, on the ILL/DD or EDD staff for the libraries in the sample was 2.07, with a range of 0 to 12. Research universities averaged 3.75 student helpers.

Mean Budget for ILL/DD/EDD Departments

The mean budget for the libraries in the sample for their ILL/DD/EDD operations, excluding staff costs but including automation, copyright, materials and other operating costs, was $14,107, with a median cost of $6,000. Costs were nearly three times higher for public than for private colleges, and were close to $28,000 for research universities; maximum spending exceeded $105,000. As might be expected, costs rose with enrollment.

Planned Changes in the ILL Budget

The mean annual increase in the library's ILL/DD/EDD budget was 2.4%, with a median of 0. The mean for U.S. libraries was 3.63% but was flat for most libraries. Mean spending increases rose with library size and the mean increase was 5.29% for libraries with more than 15,000 students.

For the upcoming year, 2009-10, budgets are expected to increase by 5.41%; most of the increase is accounted for by private liberal arts colleges, which appear to plan significant increases in spending.

Mean Fee Revenue

Mean fee revenue for the libraries in the sample was $1443.57, with a maximum of $8,300. Almost all fees in the sample were garnered by libraries that were Ph.D.-level or research universities.

Percentage of Libraries that Charge for Document Delivery

72.6% of the libraries in the sample do not charge for document delivery or for interlibrary loan and 19.2% charge to defray some, but less than half, of the total cost.

Only 4.11% of the libraries in the sample expect fees to completely pay for document delivery or interlibrary loan and to produce a surplus for the library to use in other areas.

Percentage of Libraries that Work from Unit Costs in Order to Determine Productivity Levels

4.23% of the libraries in the sample work from "unit costs" in order to determine budget needs and work for productivity. Most of the libraries working from unit costs were research universities.

Percentage of ILL Volume Accounted for by Distance Learning Program Requests

A mean of 8.25% of the library's interlibrary loan request volume from other institutions is accounted for by requests from distance learning instructors; the median was 2%. For Canadian colleges in the sample, the mean was 21.26%. For colleges with more than 15,000 students, the mean was 13.42%.

Chapter One: ILL Services

Table 1.1:   Mean, Median, Minimum and Maximum total aggregate percentage increase or decrease in traditional interlibrary loan services over the past three years

	Mean	Median	Minimum	Maximum
Entire Sample	21.29	9.50	-50.00	300.00

Table 1.2:   Mean, Median, Minimum and Maximum total aggregate percentage increase or decrease in traditional interlibrary loan services over the past three years, Broken Out by Public or Private College

Public or Private	Mean	Median	Minimum	Maximum
Public	20.88	10.00	-50.00	300.00
Private	23.57	10.00	-15.00	196.00

Table 1.3:   Mean, Median, Minimum and Maximum total aggregate percentage increase or decrease in traditional interlibrary loan services over the past three years, Broken Out by Type of College

Type of College	Mean	Median	Minimum	Maximum
Community College	36.60	16.00	-25.00	300.00
4-Year or M.A. Level	35.53	15.00	-5.00	196.00
Ph.D. Level	17.18	15.50	-30.00	53.90
Research University	-1.47	-2.00	-50.00	48.00

Table 1.4:   Mean, Median, Minimum and Maximum total aggregate percentage increase or decrease in traditional interlibrary loan services over the past three years, Broken Out by Country

Country	Mean	Median	Minimum	Maximum
U.S.A.	25.06	10.50	-50.00	300.00
Canada	3.47	0.00	-30.00	48.00

Table 1.5:   Mean, Median, Minimum and Maximum total aggregate percentage increase or decrease in traditional interlibrary loan services over the past three years, Broken Out by FTE Enrollment

FTE Enrollment	Mean	Median	Minimum	Maximum
Under 2,000	51.75	17.50	-25.00	300.00
2,000-5,000	2.94	0.00	-44.00	50.00
5,000+-15,000	24.72	17.50	-25.00	200.00
Over 15,000	9.95	0.50	-50.00	100.00

Table 1.6:   Percentage of libraries that have performed a user survey for ILL services within the past four years

	Yes	No	Unsure
Entire Sample	14.81%	80.25%	4.94%

Table 1.7:   Percentage of libraries that have performed a user survey for ILL services within the past four years, Broken Out by Public or Private College

Public or Private	Yes	No	Unsure
Public	13.73%	84.31%	1.96%
Private	16.67%	73.33%	10.00%

Table 1.8:   Percentage of libraries that have performed a user survey for ILL services within the past four years, Broken Out by Type of College

Type of College	Yes	No	Unsure
Community College	9.52%	90.48%	0.00%
4-Year or M.A. Level	17.65%	82.35%	0.00%
Ph.D. Level	12.00%	80.00%	8.00%
Research University	22.22%	66.67%	11.11%

Table 1.9:   Percentage of libraries that have performed a user survey for ILL services within the past four years, Broken Out by Country

Country	Yes	No	Unsure
U.S.A.	14.49%	79.71%	5.80%
Canada	18.18%	81.82%	0.00%

Table 1.10:   Percentage of libraries that have performed a user survey for ILL services within the past four years, Broken Out by FTE Enrollment

FTE Enrollment	Yes	No	Unsure
Under 2,000	18.75%	81.25%	0.00%
2,000-5,000	19.05%	80.95%	0.00%
5,000+-15,000	12.50%	70.83%	16.67%
Over 15,000	10.00%	90.00%	0.00%

Table 1.11:   Mean, Median, Minimum and Maximum turnaround time in days for Borrowing: Article Requests, Broken Out by Type of College

	Mean	Median	Minimum	Maximum
Entire Sample	4.54	4.00	0.00	21.00

Table 1.12:   Mean, Median, Minimum and Maximum turnaround time for Borrowing: Article Requests, Broken Out by Public or Private College

Public or Private	Mean	Median	Minimum	Maximum
Public	4.82	4.00	1.00	21.00
Private	4.22	4.00	1.00	14.00

Table 1.13:   Mean, Median, Minimum and Maximum turnaround time for Borrowing: Article Requests, Broken Out by Type of College

Type of College	Mean	Median	Minimum	Maximum
Community College	4.95	4.50	1.50	14.00
4-Year or M.A. Level	4.46	3.71	1.18	14.00
Ph.D. Level	3.99	4.00	1.00	14.00
Research University	5.19	4.00	1.00	21.00

Table 1.14:   Mean, Median, Minimum and Maximum turnaround time for Borrowing: Article Requests, Broken Out by Country

Country	Mean	Median	Minimum	Maximum
U.S.A.	4.52	4.00	1.00	14.00
Canada	5.41	3.00	2.00	21.00

Table 1.15:   Mean, Median, Minimum and Maximum turnaround time for Borrowing: Article Requests, Broken Out by FTE Enrollment

FTE Enrollment	Mean	Median	Minimum	Maximum
Under 2,000	5.69	4.00	1.18	21.00
2,000-5,000	4.40	4.00	1.00	14.00
5,000+-15,000	4.62	4.00	1.30	14.00
Over 15,000	3.96	3.74	1.00	7.06

Table 1.16:   Mean, Median, Minimum and Maximum turnaround time in days for Borrowing: Book Requests

	Mean	Median	Minimum	Maximum
Entire Sample	7.67	7.00	0.00	30.00

Table 1.17:   Mean, Median, Minimum and Maximum turnaround time in days for Borrowing: Book Requests, Broken Out by Public or Private College

Public or Private	Mean	Median	Minimum	Maximum
Public	8.70	7.50	2.00	30.00
Private	6.31	6.50	1.00	14.00

Table 1.18: Mean, Median, Minimum and Maximum turnaround time in days for Borrowing: Book Request, Broken Out by Type of College

Type of College	Mean	Median	Minimum	Maximum
Community College	9.20	7.50	2.50	30.00
4-Year or M.A. Level	6.21	6.60	1.18	14.00
Ph.D. Level	7.18	7.00	1.00	13.00
Research University	8.58	7.00	3.00	21.00

Table 1.19: Mean, Median, Minimum and Maximum turnaround time in days for Borrowing: Book Request, Broken Out by Country

Country	Mean	Median	Minimum	Maximum
U.S.A.	7.70	7.00	1.00	30.00
Canada	9.23	7.00	2.00	21.00

Table 1.20: Mean, Median, Minimum and Maximum turnaround time in days for Borrowing: Book Request, Broken Out by FTE Enrollment

FTE Enrollment	Mean	Median	Minimum	Maximum
Under 2,000	7.19	7.00	1.18	21.00
2,000-5,000	6.98	7.00	1.00	14.00
5,000+-15,000	8.46	7.00	3.00	30.00
Over 15,000	8.52	8.60	3.00	15.00

Table 1.21: Mean, Median, Minimum and Maximum turnaround time in days for Lending: Article Requests

	Mean	Median	Minimum	Maximum
Entire Sample	1.63	1.00	0.00	14.00

Table 1.22: Mean, Median, Minimum and Maximum turnaround time in days for Lending: Article Request, Broken Out by Public or Private College

Public or Private	Mean	Median	Minimum	Maximum
Public	1.76	1.00	0.00	14.00
Private	1.53	1.00	0.50	5.00

Table 1.23:   Mean, Median, Minimum and Maximum turnaround time in days for Lending: Article Request, Broken Out by Type of College

Type of College	Mean	Median	Minimum	Maximum
Community College	1.96	1.00	1.00	14.00
4-Year or M.A. Level	1.87	1.31	0.20	5.00
Ph.D. Level	1.10	1.00	0.00	3.00
Research University	1.97	1.36	1.00	7.00

Table 1.24:   Mean, Median, Minimum and Maximum turnaround time in days for Lending: Article Request, Broken Out by Country

Country	Mean	Median	Minimum	Maximum
U.S.A.	1.64	1.00	0.00	14.00
Canada	2.00	1.00	1.00	7.00

Table 1.25:   Mean, Median, Minimum and Maximum turnaround time in days for Lending: Article Request, Broken Out by FTE Enrollment

FTE Enrollment	Mean	Median	Minimum	Maximum
Under 2,000	1.65	1.18	0.50	5.00
2,000-5,000	2.32	1.00	0.50	14.00
5,000+-15,000	1.34	1.00	0.00	4.23
Over 15,000	1.47	1.10	1.00	3.09

Table 1.26:   Mean, Median, Minimum and Maximum turnaround time in days for Lending: Book Requests

	Mean	Median	Minimum	Maximum
Entire Sample	2.29	1.25	0.00	25.00

Table 1.27:   Mean, Median, Minimum and Maximum turnaround time in days for Lending: Book Request, Broken Out by Public or Private College

Public or Private	Mean	Median	Minimum	Maximum
Public	2.73	1.50	0.10	25.00
Private	1.63	1.00	0.50	6.50

Table 1.28:   Mean, Median, Minimum and Maximum turnaround time in days for Lending: Book Requests, Broken Out by Type of College

Type of College	Mean	Median	Minimum	Maximum
Community College	3.06	1.25	0.90	25.00
4-Year or M.A. Level	1.76	1.27	0.25	5.00
Ph.D. Level	1.39	1.00	0.10	8.00
Research University	3.30	3.00	1.00	7.00

Table 1.29:   Mean, Median, Minimum and Maximum turnaround time in days for Lending: Book Requests, Broken Out by Country

Country	Mean	Median	Minimum	Maximum
U.S.A.	2.40	1.27	0.10	25.00
Canada	2.18	2.00	1.00	7.00

Table 1.30:   Mean, Median, Minimum and Maximum turnaround time in days for Lending: Book Requests, Broken Out by FTE Enrollment

FTE Enrollment	Mean	Median	Minimum	Maximum
Under 2,000	2.02	1.27	0.50	8.00
2,000-5,000	2.39	1.00	0.78	14.00
5,000+-15,000	2.74	1.13	0.10	25.00
Over 15,000	2.09	2.00	0.90	5.39

Table 1.31:   Mean, Median, Minimum and Maximum turnaround time in days for Lending: Videos

	Mean	Median	Minimum	Maximum
Entire Sample	1.92	1.00	0.00	15.00

Table 1.32:   Mean, Median, Minimum and Maximum turnaround time in days for Lending: Videos, Broken Out by Public or Private College

Public or Private	Mean	Median	Minimum	Maximum
Public	2.15	1.00	0.00	15.00
Private	1.87	1.09	0.78	5.00

Table 1.33:   Mean, Median, Minimum and Maximum turnaround time in days for Lending: Videos, Broken Out by Type of College

Type of College	Mean	Median	Minimum	Maximum
Community College	2.25	1.00	0.00	15.00
4-Year or M.A. Level	2.17	2.00	0.25	5.00
Ph.D. Level	1.01	1.00	0.10	2.00
Research University	2.81	3.50	1.00	4.07

Table 1.34:   Mean, Median, Minimum and Maximum turnaround time in days for Lending: Videos, Broken Out by Country

Country	Mean	Median	Minimum	Maximum
U.S.A.	2.21	1.09	0.00	15.00
Canada	1.20	1.00	1.00	2.00

Table 1.35:   Mean, Median, Minimum and Maximum turnaround time in days for Lending: Videos, Broken Out by FTE Enrollment

FTE Enrollment	Mean	Median	Minimum	Maximum
Under 2,000	1.95	1.34	1.00	5.00
2,000-5,000	1.22	1.00	0.78	2.00
5,000+-15,000	3.48	1.50	0.10	15.00
Over 15,000	1.76	1.00	0.00	4.07

Table 1.36:   Mean, Median, Minimum and Maximum turnaround time in days for Borrowing: Videos

	Mean	Median	Minimum	Maximum
Entire Sample	6.89	6.97	0.00	21.00

Table 1.37:   Mean, Median, Minimum and Maximum turnaround time in days for Borrowing: Videos, Broken Out by Public or Private College

Public or Private	Mean	Median	Minimum	Maximum
Public	8.37	7.00	2.00	21.00
Private	5.90	5.00	0.78	17.50

Table 1.38:   Mean, Median, Minimum and Maximum turnaround time in days for Borrowing: Videos, Broken Out by Type of College

Type of College	Mean	Median	Minimum	Maximum
Community College	8.98	7.30	2.00	21.00
4-Year or M.A. Level	4.21	5.00	0.78	8.01
Ph.D. Level	8.67	7.50	1.00	21.00
Research University	6.85	7.00	3.50	12.98

Table 1.39:   Mean, Median, Minimum and Maximum turnaround time in days for Borrowing: Videos, Broken Out by Country

Country	Mean	Median	Minimum	Maximum
U.S.A.	7.00	7.00	0.78	21.00
Canada	9.75	7.00	2.00	21.00

Table 1.40:   Mean, Median, Minimum and Maximum turnaround time in days for Borrowing: Videos, Broken Out by FTE Enrollment

FTE Enrollment	Mean	Median	Minimum	Maximum
Under 2,000	6.06	5.50	1.18	17.50
2,000-5,000	5.16	4.75	0.78	11.00
5,000+-15,000	8.70	7.00	3.00	21.00
Over 15,000	8.67	7.75	2.00	21.00

Chapter Two: Shipping

Table 2.1: **Mean, Median, Minimum and Maximum amount spent in the last year for which library has records on shipping and courier fees related to interlibrary loan ($US)**

	Mean	Median	Minimum	Maximum
Entire Sample	6,856.67	2,042.00	0.00	60,000.00

Table 2.2: **Mean, Median, Minimum and Maximum amount spent in the last year for which library has records on shipping and courier fees related to interlibrary loan, Broken Out by Public or Private College**

Public or Private	Mean	Median	Minimum	Maximum
Public	8,521.12	2,721.00	85.00	60,000.00
Private	5,234.86	3,000.00	465.00	18,000.00

Table 2.3: **Mean, Median, Minimum and Maximum amount spent in the last year for which library has records on shipping and courier fees related to interlibrary loan, Broken Out by Type of College**

Type of College	Mean	Median	Minimum	Maximum
Community College	1,118.36	739.00	85.00	3,400.00
4-Year or M.A. Level	6,018.33	5,000.00	465.00	18,000.00
Ph.D. Level	5,667.75	3,800.00	650.00	20,000.00
Research University	20,044.63	15,100.00	369.00	60,000.00

Table 2.4: **Mean, Median, Minimum and Maximum amount spent in the last year for which library has records on shipping and courier fees related to interlibrary loan, Broken Out by Country**

Country	Mean	Median	Minimum	Maximum
U.S.A.	7,593.34	4,000.00	455.00	60,000.00
Canada	7,172.86	739.00	85.00	38,988.00

Table 2.5: **Mean, Median, Minimum and Maximum amount spent in the last year for which library has records on shipping and courier fees related to interlibrary loan, Broken Out by FTE Enrollment**

FTE Enrollment	Mean	Median	Minimum	Maximum
Under 2,000	2,079.89	960.00	369.00	6,000.00
2,000-5,000	4,746.50	915.50	85.00	17,152.00
5,000+-15,000	6,239.08	4,200.00	787.00	24,000.00
Over 15,000	14,843.36	4,600.00	650.00	60,000.00

Higher Education Interlibrary Loan Management Benchmarks

What criteria does your library use to determine the best shipping method for your interlibrary loans?

1. Depends on the item.

2. Borrower/lender preference.

3. Contractual agreements, destination of package, nature of material being sent.

4. Time and security.

5. Speed and cost.

6. Price and dependability.

7. Whenever possible use regional courier. All other loanables and photocopies go first-class mail unless otherwise requested (university pays for mail). PDF via Odyssey or Ariel whenever possible.

8. Existing agreements with other institutions, type of material, loan period of material, shipping cost and quality of transmission (e.g., Ariel preferred if available, faxing is second choice).

9. Price, insurance.

10. Turnaround time, cost.

11. Cost.

12. We use the cheapest method available to ship ILLs.

13. Consortial loans are shipped via regional courier, other loans are shipped first-class mail, electronic delivery is by Odyssey (preferred) or Ariel.

14. We ship library rate USPS, unless a request is made for faster delivery. Some we are able to use US Cargo, which does not have an added cost.

15. Lending -- regular mail. Borrowing -- returned UPS (tracking) or Courier.

16. Items to international locations always go USPS Global Express. U.S. locations are library rate.

17. Whatever is the fastest.

18. We use our courier service first. Then, mail or UPS, whichever can get the material to the patron the fastest and the cheapest.

19. Agreements use courier and everything else is shipped by postal service; costs.

20. VIVA lending books UPS; all borrowing books returned USPS.

21. Determined long ago.

22. The user's delivery preference(s), cost, need by date.

23. Usually expense, but will choose whatever method is fastest if time is a factor.

24. Consortium arrangement.

25. Libraries that belong to consortia, e.g., Ontario Council of University Library; Conseil des universités québecoises; American Theological Library Association, etc.

26. In Canada we use the CLA Canada Post Shipping Tool. Out of country we use Express Post Shipping, which is traceable. We rarely to never use courier. The only regular courier service we use would be a daily bin service with 4 or 5 local libraries.

27. 1. Reliability 2. Ability to track.   3. Cost.

28. Books we lend...USPS books we return...UPS.

29. If item is to be sent out of state or cannot be sent by courier or by state van, we send via FedEx. This is for tracking purposes.

30. We try to balance cost with loss / damage, ability to track and speed of delivery.

31. Cost. Only when absolutely necessary (other library policy dictates) will we use FedEx (DHL previously).

32. UPS.

33. Libraries that we have agreements with to provide items quickly go UPS. Others go via library rate.

34. 1. Fast 2. Reliable 3. Not Costly 4. Tracking available.

35. All items shipped courier for instate, USPS for out state, or FedEx based on requirements of lending library.

36. Cost and speed. Electronic delivery first choice.

37. A combination of cost, speed of delivery, insurance and tracking (when necessary).

38. Time.

39. This is determined in our mail department. I do not have the information.

40. Book Loans - UPS is used because it offers a standard $100 insurance coverage per package. They have made good on this for lost books (which is very rare).
Copies - Our IT dept. is not helpful with running Ariel or enabling email memory to handle large PDF transmission, so we send 1st class mail or FAX.

41. In-state or out of state; in-state uses UPS, out of state is mailed library rate.

42. All ILLs are sent US postage library mail unless otherwise requested.

43. Consortial agreements.

44. In or out of state.

45. Use courier service supplied by the New Jersey State Library for in-state items, otherwise we favor UPS, only use USPS if necessary.

46. Cost.

47. Default=Library Rate Mail. Special handling as requested by borrowing institution.

48. Shipping costs limit us to library rate as the preferred method.

49. At present all materials are sent via USPS. This process is currently being re-examined to determine if there are less costly ways to deliver mail.

50. Books are always sent Library or Media rate. If a deadline for receipt of material is given by the requestor, article copies are sent by 2-day express mail. They are emailed or faxed if we own the journal. If no deadline has been provided, article copies are sent by standard post.

51. We want to ship all books by UPS because of the ease of tracking the packages. The cost is similar to USPS. We send all photocopies through the Post Office because of ease of sending them out. Costs are minimal since we don't send many photocopies out.

52. In state/Courier; Out of state/U.S. Mail.

53. We sent by institutional courier to other campuses. We send by the state courier system to those in that network. For other locations, we send most materials U.S. Mail, except for Microforms or rare materials of some kind. Those we send by UPS.

54. Speed followed by cost.

55. If it's within Indiana we use the Pillow Express, a courier system. Anything outside of Indiana we use UPS.

56. Fastest method.

57. We choose in this order: 1) local regional courier first NY- RRLC (Rochester Regional Library Council) 2) statewide courier service (NYS - LAND delivery) 3) UPS (we use UPS Campus Ship) 4) USPS (all things that can't go via the top three).

58. We have a statewide courier system we default to. Out of state requests go through USPS. Sole criterion: convenience.

59. Depends on resource sharing agreement (LAND is used by SUNY System and IDS system; UPS for RLG Shares).

60. Shuttle courier for regional consortium loans; all else USPS unless specific shipping requested by lender for returns. UPS preferred over FedEx or other services.

61. University-wide decision.

62. Determined by regional office.

63. Cheapest.

64. We don't have any criteria, it will go by mail. If urgent by UPS.

65. If article, fax or email. If book, mail.

66. UPS.

67. If the borrowing library belongs to the same consortium that we do then we ship to them via UPS. If they do not belong, then we use USPS media mail.

68. Least expensive unless UPS or Fed Ex requested.

69. Least expensive.

70. Consortium agreement.

71. Fastest Method.

72. We use a consortia delivery service or UPS.

73. 1. Speed. 2. Cost.

74. Fastest, preferred method, cheapest.

75. Speed, insurability and trackability.

76. College mailroom ships all library packages first class.

77. Texshare courier (paid upfront) is preferred. For shipments to and from non-members of Texshare, we use US Postal Service.

78. Cost-effectiveness; will pay for tracking and insurance for rare items and all media; will only charge for shipping if shipped overseas.

79. Always USPS.

.

What materials and resources does your courier service distribute? Please explain.

1. Books, videos, articles.

2. Books, a/v, correspondence, other.

3. All Ontario university mail, ILL material & Media services.

4. Will handle most library-related items, i.e., books, magazines, audiovisual material, etc.

5. Courier service not used.

6. All loanable items - books, videos, CDs, etc.

7. Videos and DVDs. We are part of the MEC (Media Exchange Cooperative) which has established policies on courier shipping between members. Courier is used for non-MEC requests as well due to the shorter loan period of Videos/DVDs.

8. Packaging/labels.

9. All types of materials.

10. Books, articles and microform.

11. Our regional courier moves all loanables (regardless of format) between participating libraries.

12. We use US Cargo and it delivers all items we send through loaning practices outlined in our agreements. USPS we use for books and articles being sent based upon copyright agreements.

13. Statewide courier contract for in-state materials.

14. Books and articles.

15. Our courier service will distribute any library materials that fit in our bin - books, articles, realia, AV, etc.

16. Ship books.

17. Mailing labels, tracking services, library pick-up and delivery.

18. Mailing bgs, shipping labels, PC and 2 printers.

19. We use a provincial government courier (which is free) to send books to academic and public libraries. We will send articles via Ariel/email whenever possible. We don't use a courier such as FedEX or Purolator.

20. Envelopes, brochures.

21. Books, videos.

22. If we ever use a courier it would be for returnables only.

23. We use several courier systems: UPS, LAND (a statewide service) and some others.

24. We loan books only and will fax or email articles.

25. All materials.

26. We use Trans-Amigos Express courier service for books and articles. For micro & A/V materials, we do not use the courier service, but UPS since our packages are trackable and insured.

27. Label sleeves - we use our own boxes.

28. We use a courier service that is set up with our state library and it takes whatever we can get in the various bags.

29. N/A

30. Imprinted bags, bins, fasteners, online instructions and manifest.

31. All materials are sent through our statewide courier.

32. Not sure of question being asked....all materials and resources are shipped all ways.

33. Loans.

34. Books, articles.

35. Books only. We do not lend AV materials. That's our policy.

36. Books (Pennsylvania IDS delivery system).

37. We do not have a courier service.

38. Books.

39. Printer and labels supplied by UPS Worldship.

40. The New Jersey State Library maintains printable labels for the state with their addresses and their delivery codes for Velocity.

41. Books, media and occasionally photocopies of articles.

42. Fabric Shipping Bags Online label generation program Insurance for lost or damaged items Contractural support Online web problem reporting system.

43. In-state courier services distribute books and articles.

44. N/A

45. We don't have a courier service.

46. Anything that is shipped from a College that is connected to the Courier.

47. All the materials that we might send from ILL - books, videos, articles, etc.

48. Books, articles, videos, etc.

49. They provide mail bins, bags for shipping and plastic zip ties to ensure materials are "locked" in the bags. They also do troubleshooting for the website and are very friendly.

50. Books & articles statewide agencies.

51. Our two courier services both provide canvas bags for shipping and the trucks to get our books/videos from our library to the others.

52. All.

53. Returnables, including books, A/V, etc.

54. Regional consortium only; books and video materials.

55. Deliver all requested materials to faculty offices; deliver lending to affiliated hospitals.

56. Books, media, photocopies of articles.

57. Books/Videos.

58. All; we use Post office and UPS.

59. NA - no courier service.

60. Books and articles.

61. N/A

62. ILL, Courtesy returns, Correspondence, Memos, Flyers, Job Announcements.

63. Everything; local courier handles anything.

64. No courier service.

65. Our courier service distributes all returnable loans and occasional articles.

66. Books, photocopies, videos (in-state only).

67. Any item for the entire university up to 50 lbs.

68. Consortial loans and returns.

69. Any library materials, including supplies and some small equipment.

70. Books and AV materials.

71. We do not use a courier service.

Chapter Three: Special Collections and Unique Circumstances

What is the policy of your library on the interlibrary loan of audiovisual materials, such as video recordings, software, audio recordings and other special materials, including maps, artwork, rare materials and so on? If your library does not allow ILL of these materials, please explain why.

1. They are packaged in cardboard boxes. In the case of rare materials if a copy can be obtained within reason this is sent.

2. Will loan to libraries that loan AV to us.

3. We loan almost everything (audio recordings and special collections/rare materials are the exception) to our partners in the GWLA consortium. To others we loan a/v material and maps, but not much else.

4. Media services are currently controlled by another university department. The ILL department will lend maps to all and rare / reference material within our security transit system.

5. No ILL to prevent damage or loss.

6. AV & Special Materials = not available for IL. Loan periods too short for ILL.

7. Not loaned. AV materials are in very high demand on our campus for classroom use.

8. We do not ILL our kits. Many of our kits are custom packaged for our programs and contain multiple parts. We do not ILL them to avoid the complexity and costs of recovering lost items within the kits.

9. The material is hard to get back.

10. Our loans do not include items from our Curriculum Collection. Reason being to maximize our own student access to the collection.

11. We loan VHS/DVDs on a very limited basis. Generally upon special requests from our local consortium. Our collection is relatively small, so we are reluctant to send what resources we have away from our own community. We do not loan rare materials because of poor condition in most cases and because of value in others.

12. We don't lend these items for fear that they will be lost or damaged.

13. Typically AV materials are not loaned through traditional ILL due to high demand for these materials among our faculty.

14. We do not loan any audiovisual materials due to the replacement cost and the need for items to be available to our faculty. We do lend maps if requested. We are a small liberal arts college with limited funding for such items.

15. Our library does circulate audiovisual materials, but we do not lend materials from special collections, Master's theses or government documents.

16. Library use only with 3-week loan, no renewals.

17. We do not lend these items due to costs prohibited.

18. We loan audio, video and software. We do not lend rare items in our special collections because they are irreplaceable if lost or damaged. These items are normally for in-library use only.

19. We loan audiovisuals to academic libraries. Art, maps, rare materials, curriculum, juvenile, reference we don't loan.

20. We do not loan videos, etc., because of the cost of replacing and the loan period is too short. Our special materials/rare are non-circulating because of replacement.

21. We used to lend everything; now the policy has been changed to lend none of these materials. At the archivist's discretion, sometimes Special Collections books are loaned.

22. A/V materials, Special Collections non-circulating.

23. If these materials have a normal circulating status, we will loan them via ILL. The only time a request is denied is when the item is in high demand by our users.

24. We do not lend our videos for the following reasons: (1) High demand by our faculty and students for these items (2) Public performance rights issues (3) Length of time a video would need to be out to another library. Also, we don't lend our musical scores and compact discs (music) because of high demand by our students and faculty for these items. We will lend our software and audio recordings.

25. We will loan but only according to licensing arrangements e.g., home use only; videos don't go. More and more A/V materials are being subjected to strict licensing terms.

26. Does not allow ILL for them. Reasons: ca. 100 DVD or VHS + Library Use only.

27. We do no loan most special materials. We will loan CDs that accompany books and videos if they are available for loan.

28. We do not loan media (videos and DVD and software) because those materials are non-circulating to our own patrons. Do not have music recordings and no audio recordings of books. We do loan rare materials but have very few of those.

29. We only loan books...the chances are too great of the mentioned items being damaged or lost.

30. We loan audiovisual materials. They are to be returned in original shipping box.

31. We do not allow loans of these materials because it may cost too much to replace these items.

32. We allow ILL on video materials and software. Music recordings are determined on a case-by-case basis. Maps and other materials held by Special Collections are not available for loan due to the value of these items and the potential for loss and/or damage. Maps in the general collection are available for loan.

33. Rare materials - this is a case-by-case basis, same with reference material and journals. We try to lend everything. We don't lend M2 and M3 musical scores.

34. We don't loan. We don't have a rare book room and the other material is non-circulating.

35. We lend audio recordings to small group of academic libraries only. We don't lend other items due to concern of loss / damage in shipping.

36. Audiovisual materials are non-circulating item, so we do not lend them out for ILL. However, we borrow and allow our patrons to submit the ILL request for audiovisual material.

37. All audiovisual material distributed to Indiana Academic Libraries. Policy set by Fine Arts Librarian.

38. We loan all circulating AV. We will also special loan reference and special collection/archives material.

39. Course supplementary materials are restricted to AU student use only through licensing and therefore not open for ILL. Rare materials are stored in Archives and do not circulate due to archival policies. All materials in the general collections are open for ILL distribution.

40. Does not lend.

41. We do not lend AV materials because they are reserved for curricular needs. We do not have rare materials or special collections.

42. We do not lend AV materials. We have lent rare materials (as long as not AV). The main reason is high damage rate and the level of difficulty and cost to replace.

43. We do not lend. We do not lend to our own students. AV is non-circulating.

44. We allow everything unless it is over 500.00 and even then we might loan it out for library use only.

45. Security of materials.

46. These materials are loaned unless they are on reserve or held for instruction.

47. All audiovisual materials are lendable, except for those on reserve. Our genealogy collection is not circulating at this time due to arrangements to move it to our county library's collection. It had been circulated before this.

48. We loan AV. Rare materials must be used in the library.

49. Will loan to Consortial Partners audiovisual materials, such as video recordings, software, audio recordings and maps. ILL does not loan audiovisual materials, such as video recordings, software and audio recordings, unless they are included with a book. Reason: Fear of damage, inability to recall material in a timely manner and short loan periods (3 day). ILL will loan Maps, Special collection items & rare materials as authorized by the University Archivist. Fragile materials, artwork and sculptures do not circulate at all.

50. This material is non-circulating and therefore we do not loan. With the exception of maps and other government documents with the approval of the Government Documents librarian.

51. We do not loan any audiovisual material from our media center. We have a comprehensive music program and many of the materials we own are more expensive to purchase. We do loan microfilm church records from our Special Collections. All accompanying materials are shelved with books if book is loaned, so is the accompanying material, such as software or maps.

52. We do not allow ILL of these materials due to our limited collection, protection of copyright when used without library supervision, and the additional time and expense to ship more fragile items.

53. We don't loan any a/v materials. They are more likely to not return.

54. We will not lend out Reserve materials/special materials. The policy is Reserve Materials stay in the Library for use in the Library. As for Video and Audio recordings we do lend those to Libraries in good standing.

55. We do not loan out our AV materials except to faculty at other branch campuses of our university. Many of the educational videos are very expensive and in high demand by our professors. We need to have them available to our faculty. We will lend maps if they are available. We do not have any art that would travel. The rare materials are handled by the Special Collections department. The librarian there is concerned about the care and maintenance and safety of his collection and does not really lend any of it out via ILL.

56. We ILL videos, we do not ILL our closed stacks collection due to its condition.

57. We loan out any AV materials that are not on course reserve; our policy on most things is if someone wants it, give it to them; at least it's being used.

58. Do not lend. Policy in place when I started.

59. Our library lends all Media Materials (as long as they are not on Course Reserve or have licensing restrictions). We also lend out print journals and microforms. Rare.

60. Materials do not circulate here. We don't have maps or artwork to lend.

61. We loan AV. We don't loan anything that is for in-library use only (reference and special collection items).

62. All materials may be loaned. Through RLG SHARES, special collections materials are loaned for use in supervised reading room.

63. Regional consortium only for video recordings; rare materials assessed on a case-by-case basis - willing to scan and send unless too fragile, request too lengthy or unless copyright forbids it.

64. No ILL of rare or fragile materials; will lend videos if not booked for classroom use.

65. Library allows.

66. Local only.

67. Audiovisual materials, only when no faculty will need it within the loan time. We only do in-house use viewing.

68. We lend everything, unless it is on reserve, in high demand, or there is another "special circumstance." ("Special circumstance" usually means we are concerned about the condition of the material, but can also mean a license issue.)

69. We do not lend or borrow these materials. We do not lend current year publications. These materials are heavily used by our patrons. Our request for lending will increase since we do not charge and we do not have enough staff to handle the increase.

Table 3.8: Percentage of libraries that allow interlibrary loan of state-adopted textbooks, Broken Out by Type of College

Type of College	Yes	No
Community College	27.27%	72.73%
4-Year or M.A. Level	35.29%	64.71%
Ph.D. Level	46.43%	53.57%
Research University	55.56%	44.44%

Table 3.9: Percentage of libraries that allow interlibrary loan of state-adopted textbooks, Broken Out by Country

Country	Yes	No
U.S.A.	45.21%	54.79%
Canada	18.18%	81.82%

Table 3.10: Percentage of libraries that allow interlibrary loan of state-adopted textbooks, Broken Out by FTE Enrollment

FTE Enrollment	Yes	No
Under 2,000	50.00%	50.00%
2,000-5,000	26.09%	73.91%
5,000+-15,000	34.62%	65.38%
Over 15,000	60.00%	40.00%

Table 3.11: Percentage of libraries that allow interlibrary loan of state non-adopted textbooks

	Yes	No
Entire Sample	41.18%	58.82%

Table 3.12: Percentage of libraries that allow interlibrary loan of state non-adopted textbooks, Broken Out by Public or Private College

Public or Private	Yes	No
Public	40.74%	59.26%
Private	41.94%	58.06%

Table 3.13: Percentage of libraries that allow interlibrary loan of state non-adopted textbooks, Broken Out by Type of College

Type of College	Yes	No
Community College	31.82%	68.18%
4-Year or M.A. Level	41.18%	58.82%
Ph.D. Level	42.86%	57.14%
Research University	50.00%	50.00%

Table 3.14:   Percentage of libraries that allow interlibrary loan of state non-adopted textbooks, Broken Out by Country

Country	Yes	No
U.S.A.	45.21%	54.79%
Canada	18.18%	81.82%

Table 3.15:   Percentage of libraries that allow interlibrary loan of state non-adopted textbooks, Broken Out by FTE Enrollment

FTE Enrollment	Yes	No
Under 2,000	50.00%	50.00%
2,000-5,000	26.09%	73.91%
5,000+-15,000	30.77%	69.23%
Over 15,000	65.00%	35.00%

Please explain your library's policies on the interlibrary loan of textbooks. If allowed, what is the general loan period? What restrictions might apply?

1. We have a few textbooks and the loan period is the same.

2. Loan period is the same as those of other books.

3. Textbooks are no different from other books, but our library's policy is not to buy textbooks so it's something of a moot point.

4. The library generally doesn't purchase textbooks; however, if they are within our collection ILL would circulate based on general circulation policies.

5. We lend any book in our collection that is not reference, reserve, or part of our rare books collections.

6. Loan periods all circulating books = 28 days.

7. Treated as any other circulating item.

8. Textbooks in our regular stacks have no restrictions; they are circulated as regular material. Because they are often checked out by our students, they rarely go out to fulfill an ILL request. Other high-demand texts are in Reserves, which are not ILL-ed.

9. There is currently no policy on it.

10. We don't make the distinction between textbook request and general interlibrary loan item request. The loan period is typically set by the lending institutions (generally 3 weeks).

11. As borrowers, we attempt (some sneak through because of patron-initiated requests) to prohibit ILL for required texts for the current semester. If textbooks are not required course material, we will process the requests. As lenders, we will lend what textbooks we have for a normal loan period (60 days). We do not routinely purchase textbooks, so most of our editions are not the most recent.

12. We lend textbooks, but we don't have many in our collection.

13. Texts in the circulating collections are treated as any other ILL loan. The loan period for these is 21 Days Use.

14. We do have some textbooks and will loan for the standard borrowing time and allow for renewals if there is not a hold on the text by another patron.

15. The library lends for 30 days with one renewal, unless a patron needs the item. We do recall items that are in need by our own patrons.

16. If the material is available, we will send out through interlibrary loan. Generally, our library does not purchase textbooks for our collections.

17. We do not lend these items due to costs prohibited.

18. We allow interlibrary loan if textbooks are available. We use the same time period as other books, generally 4 weeks + 4 days. We also will renew up to 2 times if the book is not needed by someone on our own campus.

19. Our general policy is not to loan/borrow text books but sometimes it's impossible to tell if the book is a required text or not.

20. Non-circulating.

21. Loan period is 60 days; we do not have any textbooks, as far as I know; if so, they are so old that only a time traveler would want to borrow them.

22. Loans are for 4 weeks. Library use only in some cases.

23. We will loan any circulating textbook in our collection and grant the normal loan period of 8 weeks and no renewal. We will not borrow textbooks from other libraries.

24. We will lend all books to other libraries. Regular interlibrary loan periods apply. (Usually a 4-week loan, which covers traveling time.) Books are eligible for a renewal providing there are no holds on the item.

25. We don't collect textbooks.

26. Three weeks; in library use only.

27. We have very few textbooks in our collection; that is not an area we collect in.

28. The loan period for textbooks is the usual 28 days, with one renewal. We have most of the current textbooks on reserve = non-circulating, but we lend older editions.

29. Textbooks not loaned.

30. If we have the textbooks in our collection, we will lend for a period of 45 days and renew once for 30 days.

31. Yes, we allow this. Right now due to staff shortage we allow use as long as no one recalls the book.

32. As a rule, TXH does not collect textbooks. However, if we do happen to have a textbook in the collection, we will allow it to be loaned for our normal lending period of 8 weeks. We will NOT place borrowing requests for textbooks.

33. I'm going on the assumption you mean, do we lend to other libraries. Loan period 45 days.

34. We don't ask for current textbooks on interlibrary loan.

35. We feel that textbooks should be purchased by students and we don't get them on Interlibrary Loan because students refuse to return them.

36. We still allow our patrons to borrow the textbook. There is no special restriction that has been posted yet. The textbook requests are treated as regular requests. However, we realize the higher rate of overdue checked out for textbook items and are considering posting restrictions on them.

37. We no longer will lend business/marketing/finance textbooks (as determined by ILL staff and Business librarian).

38. Library materials are library materials. We officially prohibited textbook requests until two years ago, but discovered that textbook requests still went through as staff didn't identify the title as a textbook. We have instituted no current year textbook requests because of lack of availability (less than 20% full rate).

39. All course textbooks are part of our collection and available for ILL on a regular ILL loan period (6 weeks) - no renewals.

40. Loan of textbooks that are not current.

41. We would allow it with the same loan period as other books. However, we do not acquire textbooks as a general practice.

42. We lend college textbooks which may be in our collection but as a rule we do not borrow current college textbooks for our patrons.

43. Any we have are part of the general collection and circulate the same as any book.

44. Textbooks are treated like any other ILL and have no restrictions.

45. Three weeks for textbooks.

46. We don't borrow college textbooks because it is a conflict of interest with our bookstore. We do loan them.

47. Textbooks can be loaned if they are in our regular collection. We now maintain some current textbooks on reserve for in-house use only; those are not lendable via ILL.

48. Trade books which are used as texts we do borrow, but not a text that is going to be used for the whole semester.

49. ILL will attempt to borrow textbooks subject to the lender's restrictions. The library does not buy textbooks - no lending available.

50. As a policy our library does not provide textbooks to the students. We have a campus bookstore for this purpose.

51. The library does not knowingly purchase any college textbooks. If any are in the circulating collection they are loaned as normal. The library does purchase some state adopted textbooks for our Curriculum Materials Collection. None of these materials are lent.

52. We do not ILL textbooks to protect copyright when used without library supervision.

53. N/A

54. If the items are in our circulating collection, we will lend them. We do not have enough staff to determine whether an item would be considered a textbook or not. We do not routinely purchase textbooks and usually only have them in the collection if they were received as a donation. If a professor puts a textbook on Reserve, then it will not travel that semester.

55. We do not purchase textbooks and do not borrow them.

56. We do not interlibrary loan textbooks because the school's policy is that textbooks are needed for an entire semester, longer than the loan period. These items are most likely going to be overdue or never returned. Also, if it's a textbook, our students will probably need access to it so it should stay inside the library.

57. Six weeks.

58. We will lend textbooks out that are in the general collection. Anything on Course Reserve cannot circulate out to other libraries. We will attempt to borrow textbooks for our students. Lending library due dates are strictly adhered to with fines imposed if they are late.

59. If the item is part of our circulating collection, we interlibrary loan it. Loan period is 30 days.

60. Generally not done.

61. We generally don't purchase textbooks specifically because they are texts; treated as all other book loans if we have them.

62. We don't buy textbooks used on campus; if used elsewhere, we will loan them.

63. Four weeks; no restrictions.

64. Yes, if we own them.

65. We do not loan textbooks.

66. We will lend anything (that isn't on reserve, in high-demand, etc.).

67. Generally we do not carry textbooks. If it is not a current year publication, it will be checked out for three weeks and only renewal for another 3 weeks.

68. We will not borrow a textbook for one of our students, but we will loan out to other libraries any book that is not a current year publication.

69. Textbooks are loaned unless they are on Reserve.

70. Six weeks, no restrictions.

71. 28-day loan period with one renewal.

72. 30 to 45 days.

73. If the textbook is not on Reserve, we treat it as any other loan, with the same due dates and renewals.

74. If we own it and it's in the circulating collection, we will send.

75. Four weeks, one renewal. No lending of course reserved textbooks; all materials subject to recall if requested by own patron.

76. We have no policy about loaning textbooks. We generally do not add them to our collection.

77. No time or mechanism to check for textbooks; consortial borrowing does not restrict either.

78. We will not borrow textbooks.

79. We don't make a practice of purchasing textbooks but occasionally do for subject matter. We do not loan in general.

80. We may have some college textbooks in our collection, but they were not specifically purchased to assist students who did not/could not purchase their own copies.

81. They are circulated like everything else, only if they are on our stacks.

Table 3.16: Percentage of libraries whose ebook licenses allow for interlibrary loan

	Yes	No
Entire Sample	5.13%	94.87%

Table 3.17: Percentage of libraries whose ebook licenses allow for interlibrary loan, Broken Out by Public or Private College

Public or Private	Yes	No
Public	3.85%	96.15%
Private	7.69%	92.31%

Table 3.18:   Percentage of libraries whose ebook licenses allow for interlibrary loan, Broken Out by Type of College

Type of College	Yes	No
Community College	0.00%	100.00%
4-Year or M.A. Level	20.00%	80.00%
Ph.D. Level	0.00%	100.00%
Research University	5.88%	94.12%

Table 3.19:   Percentage of libraries whose ebook licenses allow for interlibrary loan, Broken Out by Country

Country	Yes	No
U.S.A.	6.06%	93.94%
Canada	0.00%	100.00%

Table 3.20:   Percentage of libraries whose ebook licenses allow for interlibrary loan, Broken Out by FTE Enrollment

FTE Enrollment	Yes	No
Under 2,000	7.14%	92.86%
2,000-5,000	0.00%	100.00%
5,000+-15,000	8.00%	92.00%
Over 15,000	5.00%	95.00%

Explain your library's policies toward the interlibrary loan of ebooks. How do you track rights for interlibrary loan? Has your library itself made requests for ebooks through interlibrary loan? Have you negotiated with publishers successfully for these rights?

1. N/A

2. Current agreements do not allow for ebook ILL.

3. We are looking at two new contracts with vendors which do allow ILL but have not signed yet.

4. Currently our license doesn't allow for lending; however, we will provide a photocopy of a section as long as it conforms with Canadian copyright regulations.

5. No ILL because of license restrictions; we are just starting to acquire ebooks, and so have not studied this question.

6. N/A

7. No effective way for the ILL staff to monitor licensing issues.

8. We do not offer ebooks for interlibrary loan.

9. Not applicable.

10. We do not request ebooks.

Higher Education Interlibrary Loan Management Benchmarks

11. N/A

12. We have not come across any situation of ILL loan for ebooks. The last check of copyright through our license indicates that we do not allow for loans via ILL.

13. We are not allowed to ILL an ebook. Unsure how that would work. Neither have we successfully borrowed an ebook. In general, our policy is to not request on records for electronic items.

14. N/A

15. We do loan ebooks through interlibrary loan.

16. N/A

17. All of our ebooks are free through netLibrary; anyone with an account could access them, and print them out a page at a time. We have never requested an ebook. No negotiations that I am aware of.

18. We do not provide access to our ebooks.

19. Don't have many ebooks and those are licensed, e.g., NetLibrary.

20. N/A

21. We don't have the licence to loan.

22. The contract does not allow for lending of ebooks.

23. We do not loan ebooks; we have not requested ebooks.

24. N/A

25. We have not tried any of this.

26. We don't loan ebooks and we don't ask for ebooks on interlibrary loan.

27. Against our licensing agreements.

28. We want to provide access to ebooks but our primary source (netLibrary) prohibits. We have not requested ebooks from another library.

29. We do not lend ebooks through ILL. Our licensing agreements with publishers do not allow ebook loan through ILL at the present time. To date we have not requested an ebook; we try to acquire a print copy.

30. Don't lend.

31. Any books for which we provide any type of interlibrary loan must be in our print collection to avoid any conflicts in agreements or copyright.

32. We do not loan or lend.

33. N/A

34. We can loan up to 10% of the book, which we send electronically to the requesting library.

35. We own no ebooks at present.

36. ILL is not involved with ebook contract negotiation.

37. N/A

38. We do not have an ILL policy for ebooks. We have not requested ebooks.

39. NetLibrary doesn't allow ILL as far as I know. That is all the ebooks we have. I wouldn't know how to send them anyway.

40. N/A

41. N/A

42. How would an ebook be able to be sent through interlibrary loan? I didn't even know this was possible.

43. N/A

44. We don't own ebooks at this time. We have not made requests for ebooks through ILL for our patrons.

45. We don't ILL ebooks.

46. Negotiate with publishers to include ILL.

47. Will loan if license allows; have a checklist of those that allow it. Don't specifically negotiate for ILL rights but this is a plus in the decisions.

48. Do not lend.

49. We don't loan any of them. (Any of the three we have.)

50. We do not ILL ebooks.

51. N/A

52. We do not loan ebooks and have not requested. We have not tried to negotiate with publishers.

53. Access is only geared toward the institution's population. We have not negotiated with publishers as we are not sure we wish to 'loan' these items.

54. We have not encountered a request and do not have a policy.

55. Circulation dept.

56. We can fill article requests for specific chapters by printing the chapters, scanning them and sending them via Ariel or email attachment.

57. Do not lend.

58. Ebooks with access only via the Internet cannot be loaned. We do not grant access to them outside our own patrons. Ebooks on CD or DVD may be loaned.

59. Have never requested an ebook for loan - have never had a request for one of ours for loan either.

60. N/A

61. This has not become a topic for our attention at this time.

62. Our OCLC Policy Directory entry states we do not lend ebooks. Since we do not "lend" ebooks, we do not allow our patrons to borrow them.

Table 3.21:   Percentage of libraries that do interlibrary loan with foreign countries

	Yes	No
Entire Sample	66.67%	33.33%

Table 3.22:   Percentage of libraries that do interlibrary loan with foreign countries, Broken Out by Public or Private College

Public or Private	Yes	No
Public	69.81%	30.19%
Private	60.71%	39.29%

Table 3.23:   Percentage of libraries that do interlibrary loan with foreign countries, Broken Out by Type of College

Type of College	Yes	No
Community College	45.45%	54.55%
4-Year or M.A. Level	62.50%	37.50%
Ph.D. Level	72.00%	28.00%
Research University	88.89%	11.11%

Table 3.24:   Percentage of libraries that do interlibrary loan with foreign countries, Broken Out by Country

Country	Yes	No
U.S.A.	66.67%	33.33%
Canada	72.73%	27.27%

Table 3.25: Percentage of libraries that do interlibrary loan with foreign countries, Broken Out by FTE Enrollment

FTE Enrollment	Yes	No
Under 2,000	60.00%	40.00%
2,000-5,000	61.90%	38.10%
5,000+-15,000	68.00%	32.00%
Over 15,000	75.00%	25.00%

What problems, if any, does your library encounter with foreign country interlibrary loan? Please explain.

1. We have not mailed any items.

2. Long delays, sometimes problems returning material to correct library due to language problems, etc.

3. None to speak of.

4. Time it takes to receive and return items, because of distance, greater possibility of loss or damage.

5. N/A

6. Only issue we run into is increased transit to and from borrowing library.

7. Shipping fees and getting the material back.

8. We've not experienced any problems.

9. We have not encountered problems.

10. Long shipping times are the most significant issue. To a lesser degree corresponding with foreign libraries can be a challenge. Thank goodness for the Babelfish web translator!

11. We do exchange articles via Odyssey/Ariel/email and fax, but have only sent books to Canada at this point. It is a long delivery process to other countries, extending the loaning period, which is possibly the reason we do not participate globally.

12. Shipping return costs and tracking.

13. N/A

14. We occasionally participate in lending articles to foreign countries, which we send via Ariel or the mail. We do not lend books, AV, or other library materials to foreign countries.

15. Articles seem to be no problem but shipping costs for books are too high.

16. No problems yet.

17. Turnaround and cost. Also, PO paperwork. In general, the book could probably be bought for what it cost to send and return it.

18. None.

19. We supply copies but no books and other returnables because of the shipping cost.

20. We very often borrow books and obtain articles from U.S. libraries. Articles are never an issue as they're usually sent electronically; however, book loans can be problematic for us. There have been times when our institution has been charged duty (by Customs) on book loans (even though the package may clearly state that there is no commercial value on the material being sent).

21. Payment of ILL with coupons; cost of ILL.

22. The length of time materials are gone from our library; this includes the lengthy shipping time.

23. We will loan to foreign countries but they do not loan to us.

24. Some minor difficulties in communication due to time differences, and some slow shipping times. Otherwise, we have not experienced problems.

25. Cost is higher in many cases, language barriers with email and with websites.

26. Long shipping time. Occasional lost items in the mail.

27. We mostly do interlibrary loan with foreign countries only for articles or anything that can be sent electronically, but not physical items like books. Since we don't want to risk losing our items or other libraries' items in the mails. Also, the loan requests with foreign countries are likely to take a longer time and likely to be very overdue.

28. Currently, we will send electronic copy anywhere in the world. We loan materials to Canada and look at other requests case by case.

29. We try to restrict our foreign ILL activity to photocopies. We purchase books if possible. When we have had to ILL returnable items, the cost can be prohibitive. The time element also influences the amount of foreign ILL we do.

30. None.

31. The only foreign countries we have done ILL with are Canada and Australia. It will always be taken on a case-by-case basis taking into consideration what the material is, mode of receipt and method of payment if cost is involved.

32. None.

33. Have not sent any to a foreign country to my knowledge.

34. Just the length of time it takes to get from place to place.

35. We have only sent items to Canada. The only difficulty has been with getting the correct forms completed accurately.

36. Payment problems due to fluctuating currency values. Payment in foreign currency not available. IFLA coupons preferred.

37. N/A

38. We do not ILL with foreign countries unless we own the material and can email the article without cost.

39. None so far.

40. None to date; we rarely get requests from overseas. We routinely lend to Canada when asked. We usually will lend theses to other countries when we have multiple copies, but don't generally lend items that can be easily obtained or purchased by the borrowing library.

41. We haven't experienced any problems so far.

42. N/A

43. Shipping is always a dilemma that arises. Packages to off-the-beaten-path foreign countries sometimes 'throw' our on-campus shipping department. Other than that we've been very successful shipping out all over the world, getting and sending materials out in a timely fashion.

44. No problems.

45. Costly to ship materials.

46. Will not lend books to foreign countries, but willing to scan and email articles. We've had minimal requests for this.

47. Cost of shipping, long return time.

48. N/A

49. Pricey shipping costs.

50. We loan books/videos to Canada. We will send copies of articles anywhere. We get books sent back for insufficient postage.

51. We used to lend to foreign countries. It took almost 6 months for us to get the books back. So we stopped lending to foreign countries.

52. None. We have only loaned to and from Canada, and we have never had any problems.

53. Length of loan required and additional cost of shipping & customs forms.

54. It rarely happens; most of the foreign requests are from Canada and they mostly want articles. Lending materials is scary and we haven't had any problems, but the fear of it keeps us from doing it. That and the cost of shipping, insurance and paperwork hassles.

55. None indicated.

56. It's been as seamless as borrowing domestically.

57. N/A

58. Paying for them. We do not have IFLA vouchers and foreign lenders do not take checks. We are wary of using credit cards for these purposes. We do not loan or request returnables - only photocopies that can be transmitted electronically.

59. Extended loan periods are necessary to accommodate shipment via USPS (otherwise we use UPS).

60. Have not had any problems.

61. N/A

62. We need to remember to change our IFM status from "$0.00" to the shipping cost to send the item.

63. International Shipping now needs to be handled on our own (no longer supported by our mailroom).

Please explain your library's policy regarding putting ILL books and e-texts on reserve for local classes.

1. We do not put ILL books on reserve.

2. We do not put ILL books on reserve, though might consider it in extreme circumstances with permission of loaning library.

3. Our reserves policy does not allow this practice.

4. We do not put these resources on reserve for classes because of control and limited loan period concerns; professors may put e-texts on their own websites for their courses.

5. ILL books are not used for reserve.

6. ILL books are never placed on course reserve. Primarily this is because of non-standard loan periods and the excessive wear and tear reserve materials get.

7. We do not put ILL books and e-text on reserve.

8. Typically it's not a practice for our library to do these things.

9. We do not place interlibrary loan books on reserve for our community, as this raises copyright issues. Loan periods would make this difficult as well. If a faculty member would like to place material on reserve that neither the library nor the faculty member owns, the library makes reasonable efforts to purchase the title.

10. We do not put any ILL materials on reserve.

11. We do not allow books borrowed through ILL to be placed on course reserve. Rationale is the unpredictable loan periods and what is typically heavy wear and tear on course reserve items.

12. We do not place ILL books on course reserve due to copyright restrictions. We must own the item, or the professor owns it before placing it on reserve for the semester.
E-texts that are in our catalog will also be linked to the course page and viewed by our students, via the e-book agreement. We do not place e-books outside of our campus on course reserve in our library.

13. We do not ILL materials returnables (books, videos, etc.) to be placed on reserve.

14. Not allowed.

15. It is against ILL policy to do so.

16. We will occasionally put an interlibrary loan book on reserve. These items are kept on 2-hour reserve and are not allowed to leave the library.   We do not interlibrary loan e-texts.

17. We won't do it.

18. ILL books are not permitted to be put on reserves.

19. ILL books cannot be put on reserve. Too much handling by many patrons seems it would cause excessive damage to books, which the library does not own.

20. Reserve services gets priority over ILL.

21. We will not borrow books for reserves.

22. We don't put ILL books on Reserve.

23. Don't put ILL materials on reserve. Loan periods not long enough.

24. N/A

25. We do not do this.

26. We NEVER place on reserve books loaned from other libraries. Concerning e-texts, the students have access to them via the library databases. We also use Electronic.

27. Reserve, but that does not apply here.

28. We will only put on reserve for a short period of time.

29. We do not put ILL books on reserve.

30. This information is handled by our Circulation staff.

31. At this time we do not allow ILL materials to be placed on course reserve.

32. We would only put ILL books on reserve if we have checked with the lending library first, otherwise we will not.

33. We don't put ILL books on reserve for local classes.

34. We feel that Interlibrary Loan is a short-term loan to one person and we don't allow them to be put on reserve.

35. This issue will be sent over to the Access Service supervisor. The copyright will be paid and the e-texts reserve will be posted at the limited time during the semester.

36. We don't allow ILL books to go on reserve.

37. While not officially prohibited, it is discouraged. We will notify the lending library and ask their permission.

38. Athabasca University does not have local classes or reserves. We are a distance education facility - our students are all over the world doing home study.

39. We prohibit this.

40. Not our policy, so no ILL books go on reserve. We do not handle e-texts.

41. We do not put these materials on reserve.

42. We do not do this.

43. We won't put ILL books on reserves but will put e-texts on reserve in Blackboard.

44. This is only done on a rare occasion.

45. We do not do this.

46. I do not put ILLed books on reserve.

47. ILL books can be put on reserve for the lending period. Faculty are discouraged to borrow books for class reserves. E-texts are made available as copyright law allows.

48. It is our policy that books borrowed through interlibrary services cannot be placed on reserve.

49. The time frame for interlibrary loan does not allow for material to be placed on reserve.

50. We do not allow materials from ILL to be placed on reserve. If a material is needed we would attempt to purchase the item for use.

51. We do not put ILL books or e-texts on reserve.

52. We don't put ILL books on reserve; we would buy the book instead. We don't have e-reserves.

53. We have not done this but if we did, the materials would stay in the Library and NOT get checked out.

54. We do not do it. Reserve items have to be items owned by our university or a private copy of the professor.

55. We do not put ILL books on reserve.

56. We do not ever, under any circumstances, allow ILL books to be put on course reserve. The only books on our reserves shelf are books owned by our library or personal copies of the professors.

57. N/A

58. ILL books we borrow for our customers may NOT be placed on Course Reserve here at Nazareth.   If other libraries would like to place our item on their Reserve we expect an inquiring phone call and may okay the practice. But we do not allow our faculty to place other libraries' materials on Course Reserve.

59. Reserve services apply only to items we own or to items owned by the faculty.

60. We do not put materials obtained via ILL on reserve.

61. Not allowed.

62. We do not put borrowed items on reserve.

63. Not done.

64. We follow faculty wishes.

65. N/A

66. We don't put ILL books or e-texts on reserve for local classes. We will buy things to put on reserve.

67. We have not done this so far.

68. We do not do that.

69. We do not put ILL books on Reserve.

70. We don't do it.

71. We do not put on reserve any ILL requested books.

72. Do not allow.

73. None.

74. We do not place any interlibrary loan materials on reserve. If professors place articles they received via Interlibrary Loan on Reserve, that is their responsibility.

75. We do not allow ILL items to be placed on reserve.

76. No ILL materials are allowed to be placed on reserve.

77. We will put ILL books on reserve only if the lending library approves such an arrangement.

78. We do not put ILL books on reserve unless there is negotiation with and approval of the lending institution. E-texts have not yet been requested for reserve.

79. We will not place an ILL on reserve unless it is an emergency to cover time it takes us to order and process our own copy.

80. We would do this in a very limited way for a short period of time (1-2 weeks, for instance).

81. We do not allow ILLs to be put on reserve.

Chapter Four: State or Provincial Borrowing Networks

Table 4.1: **Percentage of libraries whose state or province has a state or province borrowing network**

	Yes	No
Entire Sample	86.75%	13.25%

Table 4.2: **Percentage of libraries whose state or province has a state or province borrowing network, Broken Out by Public or Private College**

Public or Private	Yes	No
Public	79.63%	20.37%
Private	100.00%	0.00%

Table 4.3: **Percentage of libraries whose state or province has a state or province borrowing network, Broken Out by Type of College**

Type of College	Yes	No
Community College	86.36%	13.64%
4-Year or M.A. Level	100.00%	0.00%
Ph.D. Level	80.77%	19.23%
Research University	83.33%	16.67%

Table 4.4: **Percentage of libraries whose state or province has a state or province borrowing network, Broken Out by Country**

Country	Yes	No
U.S.A.	88.73%	11.27%
Canada	72.73%	27.27%

Table 4.5: **Percentage of libraries whose state or province has a state or province borrowing network, Broken Out by FTE Enrollment**

FTE Enrollment	Yes	No
Under 2,000	93.75%	6.25%
2,000-5,000	86.36%	13.64%
5,000+-15,000	88.00%	12.00%
Over 15,000	80.00%	20.00%

Table 4.6: **Percentage of libraries that participate in the state or province borrowing network**

	Yes	No
Entire Sample	76.83%	23.17%

81

Table 4.7:   Percentage of libraries that participate in the state or province borrowing network, Broken Out by Public or Private College

Public or Private	Yes	No
Public	71.70%	28.30%
Private	86.21%	13.79%

Table 4.8:   Percentage of libraries that participate in the state or province borrowing network, Broken Out by Type of College

Type of College	Yes	No
Community College	72.73%	27.27%
4-Year or M.A. Level	94.12%	5.88%
Ph.D. Level	68.00%	32.00%
Research University	77.78%	22.22%

Table 4.9:   Percentage of libraries that participate in the state or province borrowing network, Broken Out by Country

Country	Yes	No
U.S.A.	78.57%	21.43%
Canada	72.73%	27.27%

Table 4.10:   Percentage of libraries that participate in the state or province borrowing network, Broken Out by FTE Enrollment

FTE Enrollment	Yes	No
Under 2,000	87.50%	12.50%
2,000-5,000	68.18%	31.82%
5,000+-15,000	80.00%	20.00%
Over 15,000	73.68%	26.32%

Table 4.11:   Percentage of libraries that use state or province ILL/DD/EDD statistical reports for any purpose

	Yes	No
Entire Sample	51.25%	48.75%

Table 4.12:   Percentage of libraries that use state or province ILL/DD/EDD statistical reports for any purposes, Broken Out by Public or Private College

Public or Private	Yes	No
Public	49.02%	50.98%
Private	55.17%	44.83%

Table 4.13: Percentage of libraries that use state or province ILL/DD/EDD statistical reports for any purposes, Broken Out by Type of College

Type of College	Yes	No
Community College	42.86%	57.14%
4-Year or M.A. Level	52.94%	47.06%
Ph.D. Level	48.00%	52.00%
Research University	64.71%	35.29%

Table 4.14: Percentage of libraries that use state or province ILL/DD/EDD statistical reports for any purposes, Broken Out by Country

Country	Yes	No
U.S.A.	51.47%	48.53%
Canada	45.45%	54.55%

Table 4.15: Percentage of libraries that use state or province ILL/DD/EDD statistical reports for any purposes, Broken Out by FTE Enrollment

FTE Enrollment	Yes	No
Under 2,000	50.00%	50.00%
2,000-5,000	30.00%	70.00%
5,000+-15,000	64.00%	36.00%
Over 15,000	57.89%	42.11%

Table 4.16: Percentage of libraries whose state or province borrowing identifies Net Lenders and performs Load Leveling

	Yes	No
Entire Sample	43.06%	56.94%

Table 4.17: Percentage of libraries whose state or province borrowing identifies Net Lenders and performs Load Leveling, Broken Out by Public or Private College

Public or Private	Yes	No
Public	43.75%	56.25%
Private	41.67%	58.33%

Table 4.18: Percentage of libraries whose state or province borrowing identifies Net Lenders and performs Load Leveling, Broken Out by Type of College

Type of College	Yes	No
Community College	50.00%	50.00%
4-Year or M.A. Level	50.00%	50.00%
Ph.D. Level	22.73%	77.27%
Research University	56.25%	43.75%

Table 4.19: Percentage of libraries whose state or province borrowing identifies Net Lenders and performs Load Leveling, Broken Out by Country

Country	Yes	No
U.S.A.	45.00%	55.00%
Canada	36.36%	63.64%

Table 4.20: Percentage of libraries whose state or province borrowing identifies Net Lenders and performs Load Leveling, Broken Out by FTE Enrollment

FTE Enrollment	Yes	No
Under 2,000	53.85%	46.15%
2,000-5,000	38.89%	61.11%
5,000+-15,000	47.83%	52.17%
Over 15,000	33.33%	66.67%

Chapter Five: End User Preferences

Table 5.1: Percentage of libraries that use fax delivery in their document delivery for interlibrary loan

	Yes	No
Entire Sample	72.94%	27.06%

Table 5.2: Percentage of libraries that use fax delivery in their document delivery for interlibrary loan, Broken Out by Public or Private College

Public or Private	Yes	No
Public	83.33%	16.67%
Private	54.84%	45.16%

Table 5.3: Percentage of libraries that use fax delivery in their document delivery for interlibrary loan, Broken Out by Type of College

Type of College	Yes	No
Community College	95.45%	4.55%
4-Year or M.A. Level	58.82%	41.18%
Ph.D. Level	60.71%	39.29%
Research University	77.78%	22.22%

Table 5.4: Percentage of libraries that use fax delivery in their document delivery for interlibrary loan, Broken Out by Country

Country	Yes	No
U.S.A.	69.86%	30.14%
Canada	100.00%	0.00%

Table 5.5: Percentage of libraries that use fax delivery in their document delivery for interlibrary loan, Broken Out by FTE Enrollment

FTE Enrollment	Yes	No
Under 2,000	68.75%	31.25%
2,000-5,000	65.22%	34.78%
5,000+-15,000	73.08%	26.92%
Over 15,000	85.00%	15.00%

Table 5.6: Percentage of libraries that use email attachment delivery in their document delivery for interlibrary loan

	Yes	No
Entire Sample	71.76%	28.24%

85

Table 5.7: Percentage of libraries that use email attachment delivery in their document delivery for interlibrary loan, Broken Out by Public or Private College

Public or Private	Yes	No
Public	68.52%	31.48%
Private	77.42%	22.58%

Table 5.8: Percentage of libraries that use email attachment delivery in their document delivery for interlibrary loan, Broken Out by Type of College

Type of College	Yes	No
Community College	68.18%	31.82%
4-Year or M.A. Level	88.24%	11.76%
Ph.D. Level	64.29%	35.71%
Research University	72.22%	27.78%

Table 5.9: Percentage of libraries that use email attachment delivery in their document delivery for interlibrary loan, Broken Out by Country

Country	Yes	No
U.S.A.	71.23%	28.77%
Canada	72.73%	27.27%

Table 5.10: Percentage of libraries that use email attachment delivery in their document delivery for interlibrary loan, Broken Out by FTE Enrollment

FTE Enrollment	Yes	No
Under 2,000	75.00%	25.00%
2,000-5,000	69.57%	30.43%
5,000+-15,000	73.08%	26.92%
Over 15,000	70.00%	30.00%

Table 5.11: Percentage of libraries that use photocopy delivery in their document delivery for interlibrary loan

	Yes	No
Entire Sample	78.82%	21.18%

Table 5.12: Percentage of libraries that use photocopy delivery in their document delivery for interlibrary loan, Broken Out by Public or Private College

Public or Private	Yes	No
Public	79.63%	20.37%
Private	77.42%	22.58%

Table 5.13: Percentage of libraries that use photocopy delivery in their document delivery for interlibrary loan, Broken Out by Type of College

Type of College	Yes	No
Community College	86.36%	13.64%
4-Year or M.A. Level	76.47%	23.53%
Ph.D. Level	78.57%	21.43%
Research University	72.22%	27.78%

Table 5.14: Percentage of libraries that use photocopy delivery in their document delivery for interlibrary loan, Broken Out by Country

Country	Yes	No
U.S.A.	76.71%	23.29%
Canada	100.00%	0.00%

Table 5.15: Percentage of libraries that use photocopy delivery in their document delivery for interlibrary loan, Broken Out by FTE Enrollment

FTE Enrollment	Yes	No
Under 2,000	75.00%	25.00%
2,000-5,000	91.30%	8.70%
5,000+-15,000	69.23%	30.77%
Over 15,000	80.00%	20.00%

Table 5.16: Percentage of libraries that use the actual document in their document delivery for interlibrary loan

	Yes	No
Entire Sample	55.29%	44.71%

Table 5.17: Percentage of libraries that use the actual document in their document delivery for interlibrary loan, Broken Out by Public or Private College

Public or Private	Yes	No
Public	62.96%	37.04%
Private	41.94%	58.06%

Table 5.18: Percentage of libraries that use the actual document in their document delivery for interlibrary loan, Broken Out by Type of College

Type of College	Yes	No
Community College	59.09%	40.91%
4-Year or M.A. Level	35.29%	64.71%
Ph.D. Level	53.57%	46.43%
Research University	72.22%	27.78%

Table 5.19: Percentage of libraries that use the actual document in their document delivery for interlibrary loan, Broken Out by Country

Country	Yes	No
U.S.A.	49.32%	50.68%
Canada	100.00%	0.00%

Table 5.20: Percentage of libraries that use actual document in their document delivery for interlibrary loan, Broken Out by FTE Enrollment

FTE Enrollment	Yes	No
Under 2,000	62.50%	37.50%
2,000-5,000	39.13%	60.87%
5,000+-15,000	57.69%	42.31%
Over 15,000	65.00%	35.00%

Table 5.21: Percentage of libraries that use scanned documents in their document delivery for interlibrary loan

	Yes	No
Entire Sample	74.12%	25.88%

Table 5.22: Percentage of libraries that use scanned documents in their document delivery for interlibrary loan, Broken Out by Public or Private College

Public or Private	Yes	No
Public	72.22%	27.78%
Private	77.42%	22.58%

Table 5.23: Percentage of libraries that use scanned documents in their document delivery for interlibrary loan, Broken Out by Type of College

Type of College	Yes	No
Community College	63.64%	36.36%
4-Year or M.A. Level	76.47%	23.53%
Ph.D. Level	82.14%	17.86%
Research University	72.22%	27.78%

Table 5.24: Percentage of libraries that use scanned documents in their document delivery for interlibrary loan, Broken Out by Country

Country	Yes	No
U.S.A.	73.97%	26.03%
Canada	72.73%	27.27%

Table 5.25:   Percentage of libraries that use scanned documents in their document delivery for interlibrary loan, Broken Out by FTE Enrollment

FTE Enrollment	Yes	No
Under 2,000	62.50%	37.50%
2,000-5,000	69.57%	30.43%
5,000+-15,000	84.62%	15.38%
Over 15,000	75.00%	25.00%

Table 5.26:   Percentage of libraries that use e-text from databases in their document delivery for interlibrary loan

	Yes	No
Entire Sample	29.41%	70.59%

Table 5.27:   Percentage of libraries that use e-text from databases in their document delivery for interlibrary loan, Broken Out by Public or Private College

Public or Private	Yes	No
Public	33.33%	66.67%
Private	22.58%	77.42%

Table 5.28:   Percentage of libraries that use e-text from databases in their document delivery for interlibrary loan, Broken Out by Type of College

Type of College	Yes	No
Community College	22.73%	77.27%
4-Year or M.A. Level	17.65%	82.35%
Ph.D. Level	35.71%	64.29%
Research University	38.89%	61.11%

Table 5.29:   Percentage of libraries that use e-text from databases in their document delivery for interlibrary loan, Broken Out by Country

Country	Yes	No
U.S.A.	27.40%	72.60%
Canada	45.45%	54.55%

Table 5.30:   Percentage of libraries that use e-text from databases in their document delivery for interlibrary loan, Broken Out by FTE Enrollment

FTE Enrollment	Yes	No
Under 2,000	6.25%	93.75%
2,000-5,000	34.78%	65.22%
5,000+-15,000	34.62%	65.38%
Over 15,000	35.00%	65.00%

Table 5.31: Percentage of libraries that have facilities or personnel assigned to specifically service distance education programs in their document delivery for interlibrary loan

	Yes	No
Entire Sample	34.12%	65.88%

Table 5.32: Percentage of libraries that have facilities or personnel assigned to specifically service distance education programs in their document delivery for interlibrary loan, Broken Out by Public or Private College

Public or Private	Yes	No
Public	38.89%	61.11%
Private	25.81%	74.19%

Table 5.33: Percentage of libraries that have facilities or personnel assigned to specifically service distance education programs in their document delivery for interlibrary loan, Broken Out by Type of College

Type of College	Yes	No
Community College	45.45%	54.55%
4-Year or M.A. Level	5.88%	94.12%
Ph.D. Level	42.86%	57.14%
Research University	33.33%	66.67%

Table 5.34: Percentage of libraries that have facilities or personnel assigned to specifically service distance education programs in their document delivery for interlibrary loan, Broken Out by Country

Country	Yes	No
U.S.A.	28.77%	71.23%
Canada	72.73%	27.27%

Table 5.35: Percentage of libraries that have facilities or personnel assigned to specifically service distance education programs in their document delivery for interlibrary loan, Broken Out by FTE Enrollment

FTE Enrollment	Yes	No
Under 2,000	12.50%	87.50%
2,000-5,000	39.13%	60.87%
5,000+-15,000	42.31%	57.69%
Over 15,000	35.00%	65.00%

Table 5.36: Percentage of libraries that allow intra-library use in their document delivery for interlibrary loan

	Yes	No
Entire Sample	58.82%	41.18%

Table 5.37:   Percentage of libraries that allow intra-library use in their document delivery for interlibrary loan, Broken Out by Public or Private College

Public or Private	Yes	No
Public	59.26%	40.74%
Private	58.06%	41.94%

Table 5.38:   Percentage of libraries that allow intra-library use in their document delivery for interlibrary loan, Broken Out by Type of College

Type of College	Yes	No
Community College	54.55%	45.45%
4-Year or M.A. Level	47.06%	52.94%
Ph.D. Level	64.29%	35.71%
Research University	66.67%	33.33%

Table 5.39:   Percentage of libraries that allow intra-library use in their document delivery for interlibrary loan, Broken Out by Country

Country	Yes	No
U.S.A.	60.27%	39.73%
Canada	54.55%	45.45%

Table 5.40:   Percentage of libraries that allow intra-library use in their document delivery for interlibrary loan, Broken Out by FTE Enrollment

FTE Enrollment	Yes	No
Under 2,000	50.00%	50.00%
2,000-5,000	60.87%	39.13%
5,000+-15,000	65.38%	34.62%
Over 15,000	55.00%	45.00%

Table 5.41:   Percentage of libraries that use interlibrary loan facilities for delivery between campus libraries or units

	Yes	No
Entire Sample	47.06%	52.94%

Table 5.42:   Percentage of libraries that use interlibrary loan facilities for delivery between campus libraries or units, Broken Out by Public or Private College

Public or Private	Yes	No
Public	59.26%	40.74%
Private	25.81%	74.19%

Table 5.43:   Percentage of libraries use interlibrary loan facilities for delivery between campus libraries or units, Broken Out by Type of College

Type of College	Yes	No
Community College	72.73%	27.27%
4-Year or M.A. Level	5.88%	94.12%
Ph.D. Level	39.29%	60.71%
Research University	66.67%	33.33%

Table 5.44:   Percentage of libraries that use interlibrary loan facilities for delivery between campus libraries or units, Broken Out by Country

Country	Yes	No
U.S.A.	43.84%	56.16%
Canada	72.73%	27.27%

Table 5.45:   Percentage of libraries that use interlibrary loan facilities for delivery between campus libraries or units, Broken Out by FTE Enrollment

FTE Enrollment	Yes	No
Under 2,000	12.50%	87.50%
2,000-5,000	43.48%	56.52%
5,000+-15,000	57.69%	42.31%
Over 15,000	65.00%	35.00%

Table 5.46:   Percentage of libraries that charge a fee for document delivery for interlibrary loan

	Yes	No
Entire Sample	14.12%	85.88%

Table 5.47:   Percentage of libraries that charge fee for document delivery for interlibrary loan, Broken Out by Public or Private College

Public or Private	Yes	No
Public	11.11%	88.89%
Private	19.35%	80.65%

Table 5.48:   Percentage of libraries that charge a fee for document delivery for interlibrary loan, Broken Out by Type of College

Type of College	Yes	No
Community College	9.09%	90.91%
4-Year or M.A. Level	5.88%	94.12%
Ph.D. Level	17.86%	82.14%
Research University	22.22%	77.78%

Table 5.49:   Percentage of libraries that charge a fee for document delivery for interlibrary loan, Broken Out by Country

Country	Yes	No
U.S.A.	12.33%	87.67%
Canada	18.18%	81.82%

Table 5.50:   Percentage of libraries that charge a fee for document delivery for interlibrary loan, Broken Out by FTE Enrollment

FTE Enrollment	Yes	No
Under 2,000	6.25%	93.75%
2,000-5,000	13.04%	86.96%
5,000+-15,000	23.08%	76.92%
Over 15,000	10.00%	90.00%

Table 5.51:   Percentage of libraries whose use of Fax Delivery has increased, decreased or remained the same

	Increased	Decreased	Remained the Same	Not Applicable
Entire Sample	11.69%	53.25%	24.68%	10.39%

Table 5.52:   Percentage of libraries whose use of Fax Delivery has increased, decreased or remained the same, Broken Out by Public or Private College

Public or Private	Increased	Decreased	Remained the Same	Not Applicable
Public	16.00%	54.00%	26.00%	4.00%
Private	3.70%	51.85%	22.22%	22.22%

Table 5.53:   Percentage of libraries whose use of Fax Delivery has increased, decreased or remained the same, Broken Out by Type of College

Type of College	Increased	Decreased	Remained the Same	Not Applicable
Community College	31.82%	13.64%	50.00%	4.55%
4-Year or M.A. Level	0.00%	66.67%	20.00%	13.33%
Ph.D. Level	8.00%	64.00%	8.00%	20.00%
Research University	0.00%	80.00%	20.00%	0.00%

Table 5.54:   Percentage of libraries whose use of Fax Delivery has increased, decreased or remained the same, Broken Out by Country

Country	Increased	Decreased	Remained the Same	Not Applicable
U.S.A.	13.85%	55.38%	20.00%	10.77%
Canada	0.00%	45.45%	54.55%	0.00%

Table 5.55:   Percentage of libraries whose use of Fax Delivery has increased, decreased or remained the same, Broken Out by FTE Enrollment

FTE Enrollment	Increased	Decreased	Remained the Same	Not Applicable
Under 2,000	13.33%	33.33%	40.00%	13.33%
2,000-5,000	9.52%	47.62%	28.57%	14.29%
5,000+-15,000	12.50%	58.33%	16.67%	12.50%
Over 15,000	11.76%	70.59%	17.65%	0.00%

Table 5.56:   Percentage of libraries whose use of Email Attachment Delivery has increased, decreased or remained the same

	Increased	Decreased	Remained the Same	Not Applicable
Entire Sample	65.79%	2.63%	18.42%	13.16%

Table 5.57:   Percentage of libraries whose use of Email Attachment Delivery has increased, decreased or remained the same, Broken Out by Public or Private College

Public or Private	Increased	Decreased	Remained the Same	Not Applicable
Public	58.00%	4.00%	22.00%	16.00%
Private	80.77%	0.00%	11.54%	7.69%

Table 5.58:   Percentage of libraries whose use of Email Attachment Delivery has increased, decreased or remained the same, Broken Out by Type of College

Type of College	Increased	Decreased	Remained the Same	Not Applicable
Community College	63.64%	0.00%	13.64%	22.73%
4-Year or M.A. Level	80.00%	0.00%	20.00%	0.00%
Ph.D. Level	66.67%	8.33%	12.50%	12.50%
Research University	53.33%	0.00%	33.33%	13.33%

Table 5.59: Percentage of libraries whose use of Email Attachment Delivery has increased, decreased or remained the same, Broken Out by Country

Country	Increased	Decreased	Remained the Same	Not Applicable
U.S.A.	65.63%	3.13%	20.31%	10.94%
Canada	63.64%	0.00%	9.09%	27.27%

Table 5.60: Percentage of libraries whose use of Email Attachment Delivery has increased, decreased or remained the same, Broken Out by FTE Enrollment

FTE Enrollment	Increased	Decreased	Remained the Same	Not Applicable
Under 2,000	66.67%	0.00%	20.00%	13.33%
2,000-5,000	65.00%	0.00%	15.00%	20.00%
5,000+-15,000	66.67%	8.33%	12.50%	12.50%
Over 15,000	64.71%	0.00%	29.41%	5.88%

Table 5.61: Percentage of libraries whose use of Photocopy Delivery has increased, decreased or remained the same

	Increased	Decreased	Remained the Same	Not Applicable
Entire Sample	9.09%	57.14%	27.27%	6.49%

Table 5.62: Percentage of libraries whose use of Photocopy Delivery has increased, decreased or remained the same, Broken Out by Public or Private College

Public or Private	Increased	Decreased	Remained the Same	Not Applicable
Public	10.20%	53.06%	26.53%	10.20%
Private	7.14%	64.29%	28.57%	0.00%

Table 5.63: Percentage of libraries whose use of Photocopy Delivery has increased, decreased or remained the same, Broken Out by Type of College

Type of College	Increased	Decreased	Remained the Same	Not Applicable
Community College	9.52%	42.86%	38.10%	9.52%
4-Year or M.A. Level	0.00%	68.75%	31.25%	0.00%
Ph.D. Level	12.00%	68.00%	16.00%	4.00%
Research University	13.33%	46.67%	26.67%	13.33%

Table 5.64: Percentage of libraries whose use of Photocopy Delivery has increased, decreased or remained the same, Broken Out by Country

Country	Increased	Decreased	Remained the Same	Not Applicable
U.S.A.	10.77%	58.46%	23.08%	7.69%
Canada	0.00%	45.45%	54.55%	0.00%

Table 5.65: Percentage of libraries whose use of Photocopy Delivery has increased, decreased or remained the same, Broken Out by FTE Enrollment

FTE Enrollment	Increased	Decreased	Remained the Same	Not Applicable
Under 2,000	6.67%	60.00%	26.67%	6.67%
2,000-5,000	4.55%	45.45%	50.00%	0.00%
5,000+-15,000	17.39%	52.17%	17.39%	13.04%
Over 15,000	5.88%	76.47%	11.76%	5.88%

Table 5.66: Percentage of libraries whose use of Actual Documents has increased, decreased or remained the same

	Increased	Decreased	Remained the Same	Not Applicable
Entire Sample	17.14%	22.86%	35.71%	24.29%

Table 5.67: Percentage of libraries whose use of Actual Documents has increased, decreased or remained the same, Broken Out by Public or Private College

Public or Private	Increased	Decreased	Remained the Same	Not Applicable
Public	14.89%	25.53%	40.43%	19.15%
Private	21.74%	17.39%	26.09%	34.78%

Table 5.68: Percentage of libraries whose use of Actual Documents has increased, decreased or remained the same, Broken Out by Type of College

Type of College	Increased	Decreased	Remained the Same	Not Applicable
Community College	20.00%	10.00%	40.00%	30.00%
4-Year or M.A. Level	23.08%	15.38%	15.38%	46.15%
Ph.D. Level	13.64%	36.36%	31.82%	18.18%
Research University	13.33%	26.67%	53.33%	6.67%

Table 5.69: **Percentage of libraries whose use of Actual Documents has increased, decreased or remained the same, Broken Out by Country**

Country	Increased	Decreased	Remained the Same	Not Applicable
U.S.A.	18.97%	25.86%	27.59%	27.59%
Canada	9.09%	9.09%	81.82%	0.00%

Table 5.70: **Percentage of libraries whose use of Actual Documents has increased, decreased or remained the same, Broken Out by FTE Enrollment**

FTE Enrollment	Increased	Decreased	Remained the Same	Not Applicable
Under 2,000	28.57%	7.14%	35.71%	28.57%
2,000-5,000	5.56%	22.22%	33.33%	38.89%
5,000+-15,000	31.82%	27.27%	22.73%	18.18%
Over 15,000	0.00%	31.25%	56.25%	12.50%

Table 5.71: **Percentage of libraries whose use of Scanned Documents in Interlibrary Loan has increased, decreased or remained the same**

	Increased	Decreased	Remained the Same	Not Applicable
Entire Sample	70.27%	0.00%	16.22%	13.51%

Table 5.72: **Percentage of libraries whose use of Scanned Documents in Interlibrary Loan has increased, decreased or remained the same, Broken Out by Public or Private College**

Public or Private	Increased	Decreased	Remained the Same	Not Applicable
Public	66.67%	0.00%	18.75%	14.58%
Private	76.92%	0.00%	11.54%	11.54%

Table 5.73: **Percentage of libraries whose use of Scanned Documents in Interlibrary Loan has increased, decreased or remained the same, Broken Out by Type of College**

Type of College	Increased	Decreased	Remained the Same	Not Applicable
Community College	40.00%	0.00%	30.00%	30.00%
4-Year or M.A. Level	78.57%	0.00%	14.29%	7.14%
Ph.D. Level	80.00%	0.00%	12.00%	8.00%
Research University	86.67%	0.00%	6.67%	6.67%

Table 5.74:   Percentage of libraries whose use of Scanned Documents in Interlibrary Loan has increased, decreased or remained the same, Broken Out by Country

Country	Increased	Decreased	Remained the Same	Not Applicable
U.S.A.	75.81%	0.00%	12.90%	11.29%
Canada	45.45%	0.00%	36.36%	18.18%

Table 5.75:   Percentage of libraries whose use of Scanned Documents in Interlibrary Loan has increased, decreased or remained the same, Broken Out by FTE Enrollment

FTE Enrollment	Increased	Decreased	Remained the Same	Not Applicable
Under 2,000	57.14%	0.00%	7.14%	35.71%
2,000-5,000	65.00%	0.00%	25.00%	10.00%
5,000+-15,000	82.61%	0.00%	8.70%	8.70%
Over 15,000	70.59%	0.00%	23.53%	5.88%

Table 5.76:   Percentage of libraries whose use of E-text from databases has increased, decreased or remained the same

	Increased	Decreased	Remained the Same	Not Applicable
Entire Sample	35.29%	1.47%	16.18%	47.06%

Table 5.77:   Percentage of libraries whose use of E-text from databases has increased, decreased or remained the same, Broken Out by Public or Private College

Public or Private	Increased	Decreased	Remained the Same	Not Applicable
Public	37.78%	2.22%	17.78%	42.22%
Private	30.43%	0.00%	13.04%	56.52%

Table 5.78:   Percentage of libraries whose use of E-text from databases has increased, decreased or remained the same, Broken Out by Type of College

Type of College	Increased	Decreased	Remained the Same	Not Applicable
Community College	26.32%	5.26%	5.26%	63.16%
4-Year or M.A. Level	25.00%	0.00%	16.67%	58.33%
Ph.D. Level	43.48%	0.00%	26.09%	30.43%
Research University	42.86%	0.00%	14.29%	42.86%

Table 5.79: **Percentage of libraries whose use of E-text from databases has increased, decreased or remained the same, Broken Out by Country**

Country	Increased	Decreased	Remained the Same	Not Applicable
U.S.A.	33.33%	0.00%	17.54%	49.12%
Canada	40.00%	10.00%	10.00%	40.00%

Table 5.80: **Percentage of libraries whose use of E-text from databases has increased, decreased or remained the same, Broken Out by FTE Enrollment**

FTE Enrollment	Increased	Decreased	Remained the Same	Not Applicable
Under 2,000	8.33%	0.00%	8.33%	83.33%
2,000-5,000	33.33%	5.56%	16.67%	44.44%
5,000+-15,000	40.91%	0.00%	22.73%	36.36%
Over 15,000	50.00%	0.00%	12.50%	37.50%

Table 5.81: **Percentage of libraries whose Distance Education use of interlibrary loan use has increased, decreased or remained the same**

	Increased	Decreased	Remained the Same	Not Applicable
Entire Sample	20.90%	2.99%	28.36%	47.76%

Table 5.82: **Percentage of libraries whose Distance Education use of interlibrary loan use has increased, decreased or remained the same, Broken Out by Public or Private College**

Public or Private	Increased	Decreased	Remained the Same	Not Applicable
Public	13.64%	4.55%	36.36%	45.45%
Private	34.78%	0.00%	13.04%	52.17%

Table 5.83: **Percentage of libraries whose Distance Education use of interlibrary loan use has increased, decreased or remained the same, Broken Out by Type of College**

Type of College	Increased	Decreased	Remained the Same	Not Applicable
Community College	31.58%	5.26%	31.58%	31.58%
4-Year or M.A. Level	0.00%	0.00%	8.33%	91.67%
Ph.D. Level	30.43%	4.35%	26.09%	39.13%
Research University	7.69%	0.00%	46.15%	46.15%

Table 5.84:   Percentage of libraries whose Distance Education use of interlibrary loan use has increased, decreased or remained the same, Broken Out by Country

Country	Increased	Decreased	Remained the Same	Not Applicable
U.S.A.	19.64%	1.79%	28.57%	50.00%
Canada	20.00%	10.00%	30.00%	40.00%

Table 5.85:   Percentage of libraries whose Distance Education use of interlibrary loan use has increased, decreased or remained the same, Broken Out by FTE Enrollment

FTE Enrollment	Increased	Decreased	Remained the Same	Not Applicable
Under 2,000	25.00%	0.00%	8.33%	66.67%
2,000-5,000	29.41%	5.88%	29.41%	35.29%
5,000+-15,000	22.73%	4.55%	36.36%	36.36%
Over 15,000	6.25%	0.00%	31.25%	62.50%

Table 5.86:   Percentage of libraries whose Use of Delivery between campus library units has increased, decreased or remained the same

	Increased	Decreased	Remained the Same	Not Applicable
Entire Sample	28.57%	7.14%	17.14%	47.14%

Table 5.87:   Percentage of libraries whose Use of Delivery between campus library units has increased, decreased or remained the same, Broken Out by Public or Private College

Public or Private	Increased	Decreased	Remained the Same	Not Applicable
Public	31.91%	6.38%	23.40%	38.30%
Private	21.74%	8.70%	4.35%	65.22%

Table 5.88:   Percentage of libraries whose Use of Delivery between campus library units has increased, decreased or remained the same, Broken Out by Type of College

Type of College	Increased	Decreased	Remained the Same	Not Applicable
Community College	45.00%	10.00%	20.00%	25.00%
4-Year or M.A. Level	7.69%	0.00%	0.00%	92.31%
Ph.D. Level	26.09%	4.35%	17.39%	52.17%
Research University	28.57%	14.29%	28.57%	28.57%

Table 5.89:   Percentage of libraries whose Use of Delivery between campus library units has increased, decreased or remained the same, Broken Out by Country

Country	Increased	Decreased	Remained the Same	Not Applicable
U.S.A.	28.81%	6.78%	15.25%	49.15%
Canada	30.00%	10.00%	30.00%	30.00%

Table 5.90:   Percentage of libraries whose Use of Delivery between campus library units has increased, decreased or remained the same, Broken Out by FTE Enrollment

FTE Enrollment	Increased	Decreased	Remained the Same	Not Applicable
Under 2,000	15.38%	0.00%	0.00%	84.62%
2,000-5,000	33.33%	11.11%	11.11%	44.44%
5,000+-15,000	26.09%	8.70%	21.74%	43.48%
Over 15,000	37.50%	6.25%	31.25%	25.00%

Table 5.91:   Percentage of libraries whose Fee For Use has increased, decreased or remained the same

	Increased	Decreased	Remained the Same	Not Applicable
Entire Sample	5.88%	7.35%	13.24%	73.53%

Table 5.92:   Percentage of libraries whose Fee For Use has increased, decreased or remained the same, Broken Out by Public or Private College

Public or Private	Increased	Decreased	Remained the Same	Not Applicable
Public	4.35%	8.70%	8.70%	78.26%
Private	9.09%	4.55%	22.73%	63.64%

Table 5.93:   Percentage of libraries whose Fee For Use has increased, decreased or remained the same, Broken Out by Type of College

Type of College	Increased	Decreased	Remained the Same	Not Applicable
Community College	0.00%	5.00%	5.00%	90.00%
4-Year or M.A. Level	8.33%	0.00%	16.67%	75.00%
Ph.D. Level	13.04%	4.35%	17.39%	65.22%
Research University	0.00%	23.08%	15.38%	61.54%

Table 5.94: **Percentage of libraries whose Fee For Use has increased, decreased or remained the same, Broken Out by Country**

Country	Increased	Decreased	Remained the Same	Not Applicable
U.S.A.	7.02%	5.26%	12.28%	75.44%
Canada	0.00%	20.00%	10.00%	70.00%

Table 5.95: **Percentage of libraries whose Fee For Use has increased, decreased or remained the same, Broken Out by FTE Enrollment**

FTE Enrollment	Increased	Decreased	Remained the Same	Not Applicable
Under 2,000	0.00%	0.00%	7.69%	92.31%
2,000-5,000	5.88%	5.88%	11.76%	76.47%
5,000+-15,000	8.70%	17.39%	21.74%	52.17%
Over 15,000	6.67%	0.00%	6.67%	86.67%

By what aggregate percentage has your library's electronic document delivery cumulatively changed over the past three years?

1. Methods have changed and there is an increase.

2. +75%

3. Has been flat but now 50% unmediated.

4. Figure unavailable.

5. Increased 40%.

6. About 10%.

7. N/A

8. +5%

9. Unknown.

10. Increased by about 50%.

11. 10%

12. We have probably increased our scanning and use of software to send documents by 50% over the past 3-5 years.

13. Not tracked.

14. 80% increase.

15. It has increased by 80%.

16. Not sure.

17. 50%

18. 30%

19. Not available.

20. 10-15%

21. N/A

22. N/A

23. Increased by about 50%.

24. 60%

25. 75%

26. Greatly increased.

27. Stat is not available, but definitely a large increase.

28. We have stopped using Ariel.

29. Unknown

30. Approximately 25% increased.

31. +50%

32. It wasn't used three years ago, so all increase.

33. 18%

34. 90%

35. Unknown

36. 0

37. 30%

38. 8.0%

39. Increase minimal.

40. As a lender, we started scanning and emailing the scan in the spring of 2008. 98% of our lending is done this way as opposed to 0 in prior years. Around 80% of our borrowed documents now come electronically.

41. 100% implemented OCLC ILLiad.

42. 85%

43. 10%

44. N/A

45. Do not separate out edoc statistics.

46. +25%

47. +20%

48. 400%

49. More than 10%.

50. 20%

51. Increased 30%.

52. 0%

53. 5%

54. N/A

55. 50%

56. 40%

57. 25%

58. 15%

59. 20-30%

60. 70%, on average.

61. 100%

62. 100%

63. +8%

64. +8%

65. 44% increase.

66. 75%

67. Increase about 50%.

68. This question is unclear--are you referring simply to ILL or overall use?

69. 47%

70. 100%

Table 5.96: Percentage of libraries that have performed a user survey for DD or EDD services in the past year, past 2-3 years, past 4-5 years, longer ago, or never

	Past year	Past 2-3 years	Past 4-5 years	Longer ago	Never
Entire Sample	4.17%	4.17%	2.78%	13.89%	75.00%

Table 5.97: Percentage of libraries that have performed a user survey for DD or EDD services in the past year, past 2-3 years, past 4-5 years, longer ago, or never, Broken Out by Public or Private College

Public or Private	Past year	Past 2-3 years	Past 4-5 years	Longer ago	Never
Public	6.52%	2.17%	0.00%	10.87%	80.43%
Private	0.00%	7.69%	7.69%	19.23%	65.38%

Table 5.98: **Percentage of libraries that have performed a user survey for DD or EDD services in the past year, past 2-3 years, past 4-5 years, longer ago, or never, Broken Out by Type of College**

Type of College	Past year	Past 2-3 years	Past 4-5 years	Longer ago	Never
Community College	4.55%	0.00%	0.00%	9.09%	86.36%
4-Year or M.A. Level	0.00%	14.29%	0.00%	7.14%	78.57%
Ph.D. Level	4.35%	0.00%	4.35%	21.74%	69.57%
Research University	7.69%	7.69%	7.69%	15.38%	61.54%

Table 5.99: **Percentage of libraries that have performed a user survey for DD or EDD services in the past year, past 2-3 years, past 4-5 years, longer ago, or never, Broken Out by Country**

Country	Past year	Past 2-3 years	Past 4-5 years	Longer ago	Never
U.S.A.	3.28%	3.28%	3.28%	13.11%	77.05%
Canada	10.00%	10.00%	0.00%	20.00%	60.00%

Table 5.100: **Percentage of libraries that have performed a user survey for DD or EDD services in the past year, past 2-3 years, past 4-5 years, longer ago, or never, Broken Out by FTE Enrollment**

FTE Enrollment	Past year	Past 2-3 years	Past 4-5 years	Longer ago	Never
Under 2,000	0.00%	15.38%	0.00%	15.38%	69.23%
2,000-5,000	0.00%	0.00%	5.26%	15.79%	78.95%
5,000+-15,000	4.35%	4.35%	4.35%	13.04%	73.91%
Over 15,000	11.76%	0.00%	0.00%	11.76%	76.47%

Please list the top 5 service expectations that your DD/EDD users express to you that they need, or want.

1. Fulltext article acquisition; ILL book loans; ILL video loans.

2. They want electronic copy, fast. Sometimes quality mentioned, but e-copy & fast are main two things.

3. Quicker service.

4. Speed of delivery; location of any document.

5. Fast turnaround time. Electronic delivery of journal articles.

6. We do not offer document delivery at the departmental/unit level; we offer intercampus delivery of material. The expectations of this service are simply that 1) the material arrives within the specified time and 2) they are notified of its arrival.

7. PDF version. Electronic delivery.

8. Fast arrival, currency of material, little or no cost, personal level of arrival notification, delivery method preferences.

9. Speed.

10. Electronic delivery of documents; more than one renewal.

11. Notification of when an item is requested; faster delivery times from other libraries; more audiovisual selections available, fewer steps in ordering items—forms; more Internet delivery options/scanned doc delivery.

12. Speed, clear to read (not smeared, darkened, etc.).

13. N/A

14. They want the item(s) as quickly as possible. Electronic delivery when possible. Easy access. Easy pick-up and return. Easy request process.

15. Fast service electronic delivery of articles; finding hard-to-find books.

16. N/A

17. Faster turnaround time. Desktop delivery. Renewals on loans.

18. Speed of delivery. Ease of requesting mechanisms. No licensing restrictions.

19. N/A

20. 1.They mostly want to have faster delivery of their articles via electronic delivery. 2. To a much lower degree, they want good copies.

21. N/A

22. 1. As fast as possible 2. Correct item 3. Newest edition 4. Clear and readable copy 5. Preferably soft file if available.

23. Electronic requesting; electronic delivery.

24. 1. Speed of delivery. 2. Digital delivery. 3. High level of communication on ILL requests. 4. In lieu of ILL, alternate ways to acquire materials. 5. Support in using all aspects of the library.

25. When we started there was little reaction and they have never expressed a demand for it, although they seem to appreciate the service once started.

26. Accurate. Timely. Reasonable in cost.

27. Fast service, free service.

28. They want service that is fast, accurate, free, easy to use, patron initiated.

29. Personal Service Article Delivery - Next Day Book delivery within 5 days. Delivery of materials owned by the library. Ease of use of ordering system. One-stop-shopping concept.

30. N/A

31. We don't use document delivery services.

32. N/A

33. They expect the materials five minutes after they have submitted the request. They want a PDF. They want a physical copy. They don't want to access a cache (ILLiad), they want it e-mailed directly to them. They want a better copy.

34. Fast service, free service.

35. 1. Fast 2. Desktop delivery   3. Clean copies (borders cropped).

36. Electronic desktop delivery, home delivery purchase on demand.

37. Fast turnaround time, 24/7 access.

38. Distance Ed would like service.

39. N/A

40. Speed, accuracy.

41. Faster service.

42. 1. Faster 2. Easier 3. More convenient (pickup, access) 4. More available (we don't always go out of state for our undergrads) 5. Alternative methods, traditional or otherwise (purchasing articles from a fee based service).

43. N/A

44. Have not received user feedback.

45. We don't have any distance education students.

46. Speed.

47. N/A

48. Fast response.

49. Speed of delivery; clarity of product for reading.

50. PDFs, if possible; quick turnaround time; ease of pick-up; accuracy; thorough research.

Table 5.101: Percentage of libraries that have ever shared fulltext articles from their subscribed databases

	Yes	No
Entire Sample	65.79%	34.21%

Table 5.102: Percentage of libraries that have ever shared fulltext articles from their subscribed databases, Broken Out by Public or Private College

Public or Private	Yes	No
Public	62.50%	37.50%
Private	71.43%	28.57%

Table 5.103: Percentage of libraries that have ever shared fulltext articles from their subscribed databases, Broken Out by Type of College

Type of College	Yes	No
Community College	50.00%	50.00%
4-Year or M.A. Level	75.00%	25.00%
Ph.D. Level	69.57%	30.43%
Research University	73.33%	26.67%

Table 5.104: Percentage of libraries that have ever shared fulltext articles from their subscribed databases, Broken Out by Country

Country	Yes	No
U.S.A.	68.75%	31.25%
Canada	54.55%	45.45%

Table 5.105: Percentage of libraries that have ever shared fulltext articles from their subscribed databases, Broken Out by FTE Enrollment

FTE Enrollment	Yes	No
Under 2,000	53.33%	46.67%
2,000-5,000	71.43%	28.57%
5,000+-15,000	73.91%	26.09%
Over 15,000	58.82%	41.18%

Table 5.106: Percentage of libraries that agree or disagree that licensing agreements must be documented and followed

	Strongly Agree	Mostly Agree	Mostly Disagree	Strongly Disagree
Entire Sample	70.67%	26.67%	2.67%	0.00%

Table 5.107: Percentage of libraries that agree or disagree that licensing agreements must be documented and followed, Broken Out by Public or Private College

Public or Private	Strongly Agree	Mostly Agree	Mostly Disagree	Strongly Disagree
Public	65.31%	32.65%	2.04%	0.00%
Private	80.77%	15.38%	3.85%	0.00%

Table 5.108: Percentage of libraries that agree or disagree that licensing agreements must be documented and followed, Broken Out by Type of College

Type of College	Strongly Agree	Mostly Agree	Mostly Disagree	Strongly Disagree
Community College	63.64%	36.36%	0.00%	0.00%
4-Year or M.A. Level	85.71%	14.29%	0.00%	0.00%
Ph.D. Level	58.33%	33.33%	8.33%	0.00%
Research University	86.67%	13.33%	0.00%	0.00%

Table 5.109: Percentage of libraries that agree or disagree that licensing agreements must be documented and followed, Broken Out by Country

Country	Strongly Agree	Mostly Agree	Mostly Disagree	Strongly Disagree
U.S.A.	69.84%	26.98%	3.17%	0.00%
Canada	72.73%	27.27%	0.00%	0.00%

Table 5.110: Percentage of libraries that agree or disagree that licensing agreements must be documented and followed, Broken Out by FTE Enrollment

FTE Enrollment	Strongly Agree	Mostly Agree	Mostly Disagree	Strongly Disagree
Under 2,000	78.57%	21.43%	0.00%	0.00%
2,000-5,000	70.00%	25.00%	5.00%	0.00%
5,000+-15,000	70.83%	29.17%	0.00%	0.00%
Over 15,000	64.71%	29.41%	5.88%	0.00%

Table 5.111: Percentage of libraries that agree or disagree that it is acceptable policy to share fulltext database articles without having to verify publisher approval in every single case

	Strongly Agree	Mostly Agree	Mostly Disagree	Strongly Disagree
Entire Sample	12.16%	31.08%	31.08%	25.68%

Table 5.112: Percentage of libraries that agree or disagree that it is acceptable policy to share fulltext database articles without having to verify publisher approval in every single case, Broken Out by Public or Private College

Public or Private	Strongly Agree	Mostly Agree	Mostly Disagree	Strongly Disagree
Public	10.42%	31.25%	35.42%	22.92%
Private	15.38%	30.77%	23.08%	30.77%

Table 5.113: Percentage of libraries that agree or disagree that it is acceptable policy to share fulltext database articles without having to verify publisher approval in every single case, Broken Out by Type of College

Type of College	Strongly Agree	Mostly Agree	Mostly Disagree	Strongly Disagree
Community College	9.09%	45.45%	31.82%	13.64%
4-Year or M.A. Level	14.29%	21.43%	28.57%	35.71%
Ph.D. Level	8.33%	25.00%	41.67%	25.00%
Research University	21.43%	28.57%	14.29%	35.71%

Table 5.114: Percentage of libraries that agree or disagree that it is acceptable policy to share fulltext database articles without having to verify publisher approval in every single case, Broken Out by Country

Country	Strongly Agree	Mostly Agree	Mostly Disagree	Strongly Disagree
U.S.A.	14.29%	33.33%	31.75%	20.63%
Canada	0.00%	20.00%	30.00%	50.00%

Table 5.115: Percentage of libraries that agree or disagree that it is acceptable policy to share fulltext database articles without having to verify publisher approval in every single case, Broken Out by FTE Enrollment

FTE Enrollment	Strongly Agree	Mostly Agree	Mostly Disagree	Strongly Disagree
Under 2,000	7.69%	30.77%	30.77%	30.77%
2,000-5,000	10.00%	35.00%	30.00%	25.00%
5,000+-15,000	12.50%	29.17%	33.33%	25.00%
Over 15,000	17.65%	29.41%	29.41%	23.53%

Table 5.116: Percentage of libraries that agree or disagree that interlibrary loan staff have a defined workflow established with the staff member in charge of database licenses to verify license issues

	Strongly Agree	Mostly Agree	Mostly Disagree	Strongly Disagree
Entire Sample	29.17%	40.28%	19.44%	11.11%

Table 5.117: Percentage of libraries that agree or disagree that interlibrary loan staff have a defined workflow established with the staff member in charge of database licenses to verify license issues, Broken Out by Public or Private College

Public or Private	Strongly Agree	Mostly Agree	Mostly Disagree	Strongly Disagree
Public	19.15%	51.06%	17.02%	12.77%
Private	48.00%	20.00%	24.00%	8.00%

Table 5.118: Percentage of libraries that agree or disagree that interlibrary loan staff have a defined workflow established with the staff member in charge of database licenses to verify license issues, Broken Out by Type of College

Type of College	Strongly Agree	Mostly Agree	Mostly Disagree	Strongly Disagree
Community College	18.18%	54.55%	13.64%	13.64%
4-Year or M.A. Level	35.71%	28.57%	35.71%	0.00%
Ph.D. Level	34.78%	30.43%	17.39%	17.39%
Research University	30.77%	46.15%	15.38%	7.69%

Table 5.119: Percentage of libraries that agree or disagree that interlibrary loan staff have a defined workflow established with the staff member in charge of database licenses to verify license issues, Broken Out by Country

Country	Strongly Agree	Mostly Agree	Mostly Disagree	Strongly Disagree
U.S.A.	31.15%	40.98%	18.03%	9.84%
Canada	20.00%	40.00%	30.00%	10.00%

Table 5.120: Percentage of libraries that agree or disagree that interlibrary loan staff have a defined workflow established with the staff member in charge of database licenses to verify license issues, Broken Out by FTE Enrollment

FTE Enrollment	Strongly Agree	Mostly Agree	Mostly Disagree	Strongly Disagree
Under 2,000	46.15%	38.46%	15.38%	0.00%
2,000-5,000	22.22%	33.33%	27.78%	16.67%
5,000+-15,000	33.33%	45.83%	8.33%	12.50%
Over 15,000	17.65%	41.18%	29.41%	11.76%

Table 5.121: Percentage of libraries that agree or disagree that ILL staff have direct access to the library's ERMS (electronic resource management system) to review licenses

	Strongly Agree	Mostly Agree	Mostly Disagree	Strongly Disagree
Entire Sample	22.54%	22.54%	21.13%	33.80%

Table 5.122: Percentage of libraries that agree or disagree that ILL staff have direct access to the library's ERMS (electronic resource management system) to review licenses, Broken Out by Public or Private College

Public or Private	Strongly Agree	Mostly Agree	Mostly Disagree	Strongly Disagree
Public	14.89%	25.53%	27.66%	31.91%
Private	37.50%	16.67%	8.33%	37.50%

Table 5.123: Percentage of libraries that agree or disagree that ILL staff have direct access to the library's ERMS (electronic resource management system) to review licenses, Broken Out by Type of College

Type of College	Strongly Agree	Mostly Agree	Mostly Disagree	Strongly Disagree
Community College	18.18%	31.82%	22.73%	27.27%
4-Year or M.A. Level	21.43%	21.43%	0.00%	57.14%
Ph.D. Level	22.73%	18.18%	22.73%	36.36%
Research University	30.77%	15.38%	38.46%	15.38%

Table 5.124: Percentage of libraries that agree or disagree that ILL staff have direct access to the library's ERMS (electronic resource management system) to review licenses, Broken Out by Country

Country	Strongly Agree	Mostly Agree	Mostly Disagree	Strongly Disagree
U.S.A.	21.67%	25.00%	20.00%	33.33%
Canada	30.00%	10.00%	30.00%	30.00%

Table 5.125: Percentage of libraries that agree or disagree that ILL staff have direct access to the library's ERMS (electronic resource management system) to review licenses, Broken Out by FTE Enrollment

FTE Enrollment	Strongly Agree	Mostly Agree	Mostly Disagree	Strongly Disagree
Under 2,000	30.77%	23.08%	15.38%	30.77%
2,000-5,000	23.53%	17.65%	23.53%	35.29%
5,000+-15,000	20.83%	29.17%	16.67%	33.33%
Over 15,000	17.65%	17.65%	29.41%	35.29%

Table 5.126: Percentage of libraries that agree or disagree that License issue questions are handled on an ad hoc basis, as needed, without written practices

	Strongly Agree	Mostly Agree	Mostly Disagree	Strongly Disagree
Entire Sample	12.86%	42.86%	22.86%	21.43%

Table 5.127: Percentage of libraries that agree or disagree that License issue questions are handled on an ad hoc basis, as needed, without written practices, Broken Out by Public or Private College

Public or Private	Strongly Agree	Mostly Agree	Mostly Disagree	Strongly Disagree
Public	8.51%	44.68%	23.40%	23.40%
Private	21.74%	39.13%	21.74%	17.39%

Table 5.128: Percentage of libraries that agree or disagree that License issue questions are handled on an ad hoc basis, as needed, without written practices, Broken Out by Type of College

Type of College	Strongly Agree	Mostly Agree	Mostly Disagree	Strongly Disagree
Community College	4.55%	36.36%	31.82%	27.27%
4-Year or M.A. Level	35.71%	28.57%	21.43%	14.29%
Ph.D. Level	0.00%	63.64%	13.64%	22.73%
Research University	25.00%	33.33%	25.00%	16.67%

Table 5.129: Percentage of libraries that agree or disagree that License issue questions are handled on an ad hoc basis, as needed, without written practices, Broken Out by Country

Country	Strongly Agree	Mostly Agree	Mostly Disagree	Strongly Disagree
U.S.A.	12.07%	46.55%	22.41%	18.97%
Canada	18.18%	27.27%	27.27%	27.27%

Table 5.130: Percentage of libraries that agree or disagree that License issue questions are handled on an ad hoc basis, as needed, without written practices, Broken Out by FTE Enrollment

FTE Enrollment	Strongly Agree	Mostly Agree	Mostly Disagree	Strongly Disagree
Under 2,000	21.43%	35.71%	35.71%	7.14%
2,000-5,000	23.53%	41.18%	11.76%	23.53%
5,000+-15,000	0.00%	45.45%	27.27%	27.27%
Over 15,000	11.76%	47.06%	17.65%	23.53%

Table 5.131: Percentage of libraries that agree or disagree that Maintaining license agreements is handled in the Library by Acquisitions staff

	Strongly Agree	Mostly Agree	Mostly Disagree	Strongly Disagree
Entire Sample	34.72%	29.17%	8.33%	27.78%

Table 5.132: Percentage of libraries that agree or disagree that Maintaining license agreements is handled in the Library by Acquisitions staff, Broken Out by Public or Private College

Public or Private	Strongly Agree	Mostly Agree	Mostly Disagree	Strongly Disagree
Public	38.78%	28.57%	8.16%	24.49%
Private	26.09%	30.43%	8.70%	34.78%

114

Table 5.133: Percentage of libraries that agree or disagree that Maintaining license agreements is handled in the Library by Acquisitions staff, Broken Out by Type of College

Type of College	Strongly Agree	Mostly Agree	Mostly Disagree	Strongly Disagree
Community College	27.27%	36.36%	9.09%	27.27%
4-Year or M.A. Level	21.43%	42.86%	14.29%	21.43%
Ph.D. Level	39.13%	21.74%	8.70%	30.43%
Research University	53.85%	15.38%	0.00%	30.77%

Table 5.134: Percentage of libraries that agree or disagree that Maintaining license agreements is handled in the Library by Acquisitions staff, Broken Out by Country

Country	Strongly Agree	Mostly Agree	Mostly Disagree	Strongly Disagree
U.S.A.	36.67%	28.33%	10.00%	25.00%
Canada	27.27%	36.36%	0.00%	36.36%

Table 5.135: Percentage of libraries that agree or disagree that Maintaining license agreements is handled in the Library by Acquisitions staff, Broken Out by FTE Enrollment

FTE Enrollment	Strongly Agree	Mostly Agree	Mostly Disagree	Strongly Disagree
Under 2,000	21.43%	35.71%	14.29%	28.57%
2,000-5,000	36.84%	21.05%	5.26%	36.84%
5,000+-15,000	40.91%	31.82%	9.09%	18.18%
Over 15,000	35.29%	29.41%	5.88%	29.41%

Chapter Six: Departmental Responsibility

Table 6.1: **Percentage of libraries whose Interlibrary Loan and Document Delivery Services are performed largely by the same library unit or by separate units**

	Largely by the same unit	Separate units
Entire Sample	91.67%	8.33%

Table 6.2: **Percentage of libraries whose Interlibrary Loan and Document Delivery Services are performed largely by the same library unit or by separate units, Broken Out by Public or Private College**

Public or Private	Largely by the same unit	Separate units
Public	93.75%	6.25%
Private	87.50%	12.50%

Table 6.3: **Percentage of libraries whose Interlibrary Loan and Document Delivery Services are performed largely by the same library unit or by separate units, Broken Out by Type of College**

Type of College	Largely by the same unit	Separate units
Community College	95.45%	4.55%
4-Year or M.A. Level	93.33%	6.67%
Ph.D. Level	86.96%	13.04%
Research University	91.67%	8.33%

Table 6.4: **Percentage of libraries whose Interlibrary Loan and Document Delivery Services are performed largely by the same library unit or by separate units, Broken Out by Country**

Country	Largely by the same unit	Separate units
U.S.A.	91.80%	8.20%
Canada	90.00%	10.00%

Table 6.5: **Percentage of libraries whose Interlibrary Loan and Document Delivery Services are performed largely by the same library unit or by separate units, Broken Out by FTE Enrollment**

FTE Enrollment	Largely by the same unit	Separate units
Under 2,000	92.86%	7.14%
2,000-5,000	89.47%	10.53%
5,000+-15,000	90.91%	9.09%
Over 15,000	94.12%	5.88%

Table 6.6: **Percentage of libraries where ILL is under the auspices of the Reference Department**

	Yes	No
Entire Sample	21.18%	78.82%

Table 6.7: **Percentage of libraries where ILL is under the auspices of the Reference Department, Broken Out by Public or Private College**

Public or Private	Yes	No
Public	22.22%	77.78%
Private	19.35%	80.65%

Table 6.8: **Percentage of libraries where ILL is under the auspices of the Reference Department, Broken Out by Type of College**

Type of College	Yes	No
Community College	31.82%	68.18%
4-Year or M.A. Level	23.53%	76.47%
Ph.D. Level	10.71%	89.29%
Research University	22.22%	77.78%

Table 6.9: **Percentage of libraries where ILL is under the auspices of the Reference Department, Broken Out by Country**

Country	Yes	No
U.S.A.	19.18%	80.82%
Canada	36.36%	63.64%

Table 6.10: **Percentage of libraries where ILL is under the auspices of the Reference Department, Broken Out by FTE Enrollment**

FTE Enrollment	Yes	No
Under 2,000	31.25%	68.75%
2,000-5,000	21.74%	78.26%
5,000+-15,000	23.08%	76.92%
Over 15,000	10.00%	90.00%

Table 6.11: **Percentage of libraries where ILL is under the auspices of the Circulation Department**

	Yes	No
Entire Sample	28.24%	71.76%

Table 6.12: **Percentage of libraries where ILL is under the auspices of the Circulation Department, Broken Out by Public or Private College**

Public or Private	Yes	No
Public	29.63%	70.37%
Private	25.81%	74.19%

117

Table 6.13: Percentage of libraries where ILL is under the auspices of the Circulation Department, Broken Out by Type of College

Type of College	Yes	No
Community College	40.91%	59.09%
4-Year or M.A. Level	29.41%	70.59%
Ph.D. Level	17.86%	82.14%
Research University	27.78%	72.22%

Table 6.14: Percentage of libraries where ILL is under the auspices of the Circulation Department, Broken Out by Country

Country	Yes	No
U.S.A.	28.77%	71.23%
Canada	27.27%	72.73%

Table 6.15: Percentage of libraries where ILL is under the auspices of the Circulation Department, Broken Out by FTE Enrollment

FTE Enrollment	Yes	No
Under 2,000	50.00%	50.00%
2,000-5,000	17.39%	82.61%
5,000+-15,000	26.92%	73.08%
Over 15,000	25.00%	75.00%

Table 6.16: Percentage of libraries where ILL is under the auspices of the Access Services Department

	Yes	No
Entire Sample	21.18%	78.82%

Table 6.17: Percentage of libraries where ILL is under the auspices of the Access Services Department, Broken Out by Public or Private College

Public or Private	Yes	No
Public	20.37%	79.63%
Private	22.58%	77.42%

Table 6.18: Percentage of libraries where ILL is under the auspices of the Access Services Department, Broken Out by Type of College

Type of College	Yes	No
Community College	9.09%	90.91%
4-Year or M.A. Level	23.53%	76.47%
Ph.D. Level	25.00%	75.00%
Research University	27.78%	72.22%

Table 6.19:   Percentage of libraries where ILL is under the auspices of the Access Services Department, Broken Out by Country

Country	Yes	No
U.S.A.	24.66%	75.34%
Canada	0.00%	100.00%

Table 6.20:   Percentage of libraries where ILL is under the auspices of the Access Services Department, Broken Out by FTE Enrollment

FTE Enrollment	Yes	No
Under 2,000	12.50%	87.50%
2,000-5,000	17.39%	82.61%
5,000+-15,000	26.92%	73.08%
Over 15,000	25.00%	75.00%

Table 6.21:   Percentage of libraries where ILL is under the auspices of the Document Delivery Services Department

	Yes	No
Entire Sample	21.18%	78.82%

Table 6.22:   Percentage of libraries where ILL is under the auspices of the Document Delivery Services Department, Broken Out by Public or Private College

Public or Private	Yes	No
Public	20.37%	79.63%
Private	22.58%	77.42%

Table 6.23:   Percentage of libraries where ILL is under the auspices of the Document Delivery Services Department, Broken Out by Type of College

Type of College	Yes	No
Community College	9.09%	90.91%
4-Year or M.A. Level	23.53%	76.47%
Ph.D. Level	25.00%	75.00%
Research University	27.78%	72.22%

Table 6.24:   Percentage of libraries where ILL is under the auspices of the Document Delivery Services Department, Broken Out by Country

Country	Yes	No
U.S.A.	24.66%	75.34%
Canada	0.00%	100.00%

Table 6.25: Percentage of libraries where ILL is under the auspices of the Document Delivery Services Department, Broken Out by FTE Enrollment

FTE Enrollment	Yes	No
Under 2,000	12.50%	87.50%
2,000-5,000	17.39%	82.61%
5,000+-15,000	26.92%	73.08%
Over 15,000	25.00%	75.00%

Table 6.26: Percentage of libraries where ILL is under the auspices of the Technical Services Department

	Yes	No
Entire Sample	12.94%	87.06%

Table 6.27: Percentage of libraries where ILL is under the auspices of the Technical Services Department, Broken Out by Public or Private College

Public or Private	Yes	No
Public	18.52%	81.48%
Private	3.23%	96.77%

Table 6.28: Percentage of libraries where ILL is under the auspices of the Technical Services Department, Broken Out by Type of College

Type of College	Yes	No
Community College	13.64%	86.36%
4-Year or M.A. Level	5.88%	94.12%
Ph.D. Level	21.43%	78.57%
Research University	5.56%	94.44%

Table 6.29: Percentage of libraries where ILL is under the auspices of the Technical Services Department, Broken Out by Country

Country	Yes	No
U.S.A.	10.96%	89.04%
Canada	27.27%	72.73%

Table 6.30: Percentage of libraries where ILL is under the auspices of the Technical Services Department, Broken Out by FTE Enrollment

FTE Enrollment	Yes	No
Under 2,000	12.50%	87.50%
2,000-5,000	13.04%	86.96%
5,000+-15,000	15.38%	84.62%
Over 15,000	10.00%	90.00%

Table 6.31:   Percentage of libraries where ILL is under the auspices of the Collection Development Department

	Yes	No
Entire Sample	11.76%	88.24%

Table 6.32:   Percentage of libraries where ILL is under the auspices of the Collection Development Department, Broken Out by Public or Private College

Public or Private	Yes	No
Public	14.81%	85.19%
Private	6.45%	93.55%

Table 6.33:   Percentage of libraries where ILL is under the auspices of the Collection Development Department, Broken Out by Type of College

Type of College	Yes	No
Community College	27.27%	72.73%
4-Year or M.A. Level	11.76%	88.24%
Ph.D. Level	7.14%	92.86%
Research University	0.00%	100.00%

Table 6.34:   Percentage of libraries where ILL is under the auspices of the Collection Development Department, Broken Out by Country

Country	Yes	No
U.S.A.	12.33%	87.67%
Canada	9.09%	90.91%

Table 6.35:   Percentage of libraries where ILL is under the auspices of the Collection Development Department, Broken Out by FTE Enrollment

FTE Enrollment	Yes	No
Under 2,000	12.50%	87.50%
2,000-5,000	17.39%	82.61%
5,000+-15,000	11.54%	88.46%
Over 15,000	5.00%	95.00%

Table 6.36:   Percentage of libraries where ILL is under the auspices of another department not previously cited above

	Yes	No
Entire Sample	21.18%	78.82%

Table 6.37: Percentage of libraries where ILL is under the auspices of another department not previously cited above, Broken Out by Public or Private College

Public or Private	Yes	No
Public	18.52%	81.48%
Private	25.81%	74.19%

Table 6.38: Percentage of libraries where ILL is under the auspices of another department not previously cited above, Broken Out by Type of College

Type of College	Yes	No
Community College	18.18%	81.82%
4-Year or M.A. Level	11.76%	88.24%
Ph.D. Level	32.14%	67.86%
Research University	16.67%	83.33%

Table 6.39: Percentage of libraries where ILL is under the auspices of another department not previously cited above, Broken Out by Country

Country	Yes	No
U.S.A.	20.55%	79.45%
Canada	18.18%	81.82%

Table 6.40: Percentage of libraries where ILL is under the auspices of another department not previously cited above, Broken Out by FTE Enrollment

FTE Enrollment	Yes	No
Under 2,000	18.75%	81.25%
2,000-5,000	17.39%	82.61%
5,000+-15,000	23.08%	76.92%
Over 15,000	25.00%	75.00%

Table 6.41: Percentage of libraries where DD/EDD is under the auspices of the Reference Department

	Yes	No
Entire Sample	21.18%	78.82%

Table 6.42: Percentage of libraries where DD/EDD is under the auspices of the Reference Department, Broken Out by Public or Private College

Public or Private	Yes	No
Public	24.07%	75.93%
Private	16.13%	83.87%

Table 6.43:   Percentage of libraries where DD/EDD is under the auspices of the Reference Department, Broken Out by Type of College

Type of College	Yes	No
Community College	40.91%	59.09%
4-Year or M.A. Level	23.53%	76.47%
Ph.D. Level	7.14%	92.86%
Research University	16.67%	83.33%

Table 6.44:   Percentage of libraries where DD/EDD is under the auspices of the Reference Department, Broken Out by Country

Country	Yes	No
U.S.A.	17.81%	82.19%
Canada	45.45%	54.55%

Table 6.45:   Percentage of libraries where DD/EDD is under the auspices of the Reference Department, Broken Out by FTE Enrollment

FTE Enrollment	Yes	No
Under 2,000	37.50%	62.50%
2,000-5,000	21.74%	78.26%
5,000+-15,000	11.54%	88.46%
Over 15,000	20.00%	80.00%

Table 6.46:   Percentage of libraries where DD/EDD is under the auspices of the Circulation Department

	Yes	No
Entire Sample	20.00%	80.00%

Table 6.47:   Percentage of libraries where DD/EDD is under the auspices of the Circulation Department, Broken Out by Public or Private College

Public or Private	Yes	No
Public	22.22%	77.78%
Private	16.13%	83.87%

Table 6.48:   Percentage of libraries where DD/EDD is under the auspices of the Circulation Department, Broken Out by Type of College

Type of College	Yes	No
Community College	36.36%	63.64%
4-Year or M.A. Level	23.53%	76.47%
Ph.D. Level	3.57%	96.43%
Research University	22.22%	77.78%

Table 6.49: **Percentage of libraries where DD/EDD is under the auspices of the Circulation Department, Broken Out by Country**

Country	Yes	No
U.S.A.	19.18%	80.82%
Canada	27.27%	72.73%

Table 6.50: **Percentage of libraries where DD/EDD is under the auspices of the Circulation Department, Broken Out by FTE Enrollment**

FTE Enrollment	Yes	No
Under 2,000	43.75%	56.25%
2,000-5,000	13.04%	86.96%
5,000+-15,000	15.38%	84.62%
Over 15,000	15.00%	85.00%

Table 6.51: **Percentage of libraries where DD/EDD is under the auspices of the Access Services Department**

	Yes	No
Entire Sample	17.65%	82.35%

Table 6.52: **Percentage of libraries where DD/EDD is under the auspices of the Access Services Department, Broken Out by Public or Private College**

Public or Private	Yes	No
Public	16.67%	83.33%
Private	19.35%	80.65%

Table 6.53: **Percentage of libraries where DD/EDD is under the auspices of the Access Services Department, Broken Out by Type of College**

Type of College	Yes	No
Community College	9.09%	90.91%
4-Year or M.A. Level	11.76%	88.24%
Ph.D. Level	21.43%	78.57%
Research University	27.78%	72.22%

Table 6.54: **Percentage of libraries where DD/EDD is under the auspices of the Access Services Department, Broken Out by Country**

Country	Yes	No
U.S.A.	20.55%	79.45%
Canada	0.00%	100.00%

Table 6.55:   Percentage of libraries where DD/EDD is under the auspices of the Access Services Department, Broken Out by FTE Enrollment

FTE Enrollment	Yes	No
Under 2,000	12.50%	87.50%
2,000-5,000	13.04%	86.96%
5,000+-15,000	23.08%	76.92%
Over 15,000	20.00%	80.00%

Table 6.56:   Percentage of libraries where DD/EDD is under the auspices of the Document Delivery Services Department

	Yes	No
Entire Sample	7.06%	92.94%

Table 6.57:   Percentage of libraries where DD/EDD is under the auspices of the Document Delivery Services Department, Broken Out by Public or Private College

Public or Private	Yes	No
Public	11.11%	88.89%
Private	0.00%	100.00%

Table 6.58:   Percentage of libraries where DD/EDD is under the auspices of the Document Delivery Services Department, Broken Out by Type of College

Type of College	Yes	No
Community College	9.09%	90.91%
4-Year or M.A. Level	5.88%	94.12%
Ph.D. Level	10.71%	89.29%
Research University	0.00%	100.00%

Table 6.59:   Percentage of libraries where DD/EDD is under the auspices of the Document Delivery Services Department, Broken Out by Country

Country	Yes	No
U.S.A.	5.48%	94.52%
Canada	18.18%	81.82%

Table 6.60:   Percentage of libraries where DD/EDD is under the auspices of the Document Delivery Services Department, Broken Out by FTE Enrollment

FTE Enrollment	Yes	No
Under 2,000	6.25%	93.75%
2,000-5,000	8.70%	91.30%
5,000+-15,000	11.54%	88.46%
Over 15,000	0.00%	100.00%

Table 6.61: **Percentage of libraries where DD/EDD is under the auspices of the Technical Services Department**

	Yes	No
Entire Sample	9.41%	90.59%

Table 6.62: **Percentage of libraries where DD/EDD is under the auspices of the Technical Services Department, Broken Out by Public or Private College**

Public or Private	Yes	No
Public	11.11%	88.89%
Private	6.45%	93.55%

Table 6.63: **Percentage of libraries where DD/EDD is under the auspices of the Technical Services Department, Broken Out by Type of College**

Type of College	Yes	No
Community College	22.73%	77.27%
4-Year or M.A. Level	11.76%	88.24%
Ph.D. Level	3.57%	96.43%
Research University	0.00%	100.00%

Table 6.64: **Percentage of libraries where DD/EDD is under the auspices of the Technical Services Department, Broken Out by Country**

Country	Yes	No
U.S.A.	9.59%	90.41%
Canada	9.09%	90.91%

Table 6.65: **Percentage of libraries where DD/EDD is under the auspices of the Technical Services Department, Broken Out by FTE Enrollment**

FTE Enrollment	Yes	No
Under 2,000	12.50%	87.50%
2,000-5,000	13.04%	86.96%
5,000+-15,000	7.69%	92.31%
Over 15,000	5.00%	95.00%

Table 6.66: **Percentage of libraries where DD/EDD is under the auspices of the Collection Development Department**

	Yes	No
Entire Sample	1.18%	98.82%

Table 6.67:   Percentage of libraries where DD/EDD is under the auspices of the Collection Development Department, Broken Out by Public or Private College

Public or Private	Yes	No
Public	1.85%	98.15%
Private	0.00%	100.00%

Table 6.68:   Percentage of libraries where DD/EDD is under the auspices of the Collection Development Department, Broken Out by Type of College

Type of College	Yes	No
Community College	4.55%	95.45%
4-Year or M.A. Level	0.00%	100.00%
Ph.D. Level	0.00%	100.00%
Research University	0.00%	100.00%

Table 6.69:   Percentage of libraries where DD/EDD is under the auspices of the Collection Development Department, Broken Out by Country

Country	Yes	No
U.S.A.	1.37%	98.63%
Canada	0.00%	100.00%

Table 6.70:   Percentage of libraries where DD/EDD is under the auspices of the Collection Development Department, Broken Out by FTE Enrollment

FTE Enrollment	Yes	No
Under 2,000	6.25%	93.75%
2,000-5,000	0.00%	100.00%
5,000+-15,000	0.00%	100.00%
Over 15,000	0.00%	100.00%

Table 6.71:   Percentage of libraries where DD/EDD is under the auspices of another department not previously cited above

	Yes	No
Entire Sample	24.71%	75.29%

Table 6.72:   Percentage of libraries where DD/EDD is under the auspices of another department not previously cited above, Broken Out by Public or Private College

Public or Private	Yes	No
Public	20.37%	79.63%
Private	32.26%	67.74%

Table 6.73: **Percentage of libraries where DD/EDD is under the auspices of another department not previously cited above, Broken Out by Type of College**

Type of College	Yes	No
Community College	18.18%	81.82%
4-Year or M.A. Level	23.53%	76.47%
Ph.D. Level	35.71%	64.29%
Research University	16.67%	83.33%

Table 6.74: **Percentage of libraries where DD/EDD is under the auspices of another department not previously cited above, Broken Out by Country**

Country	Yes	No
U.S.A.	24.66%	75.34%
Canada	18.18%	81.82%

Table 6.75: **Percentage of libraries where DD/EDD is under the auspices of another department not previously cited above, Broken Out by FTE Enrollment**

FTE Enrollment	Yes	No
Under 2,000	18.75%	81.25%
2,000-5,000	17.39%	82.61%
5,000+-15,000	34.62%	65.38%
Over 15,000	25.00%	75.00%

Table 6.76: **Percentage of libraries where Circulation Department handles any part of ILL/DD/EDD**

	Yes	No
Entire Sample	67.57%	32.43%

Table 6.77: **Percentage of libraries where Circulation Department handles any part of ILL/DD/EDD, Broken Out by Public or Private College**

Public or Private	Yes	No
Public	70.83%	29.17%
Private	61.54%	38.46%

Table 6.78: **Percentage of libraries where Circulation Department handles any part of ILL/DD/EDD, Broken Out by Type of College**

Type of College	Yes	No
Community College	72.73%	27.27%
4-Year or M.A. Level	60.00%	40.00%
Ph.D. Level	60.87%	39.13%
Research University	78.57%	21.43%

Table 6.79: **Percentage of libraries where Circulation Department handles any part of ILL/DD/EDD, Broken Out by Country**

Country	Yes	No
U.S.A.	65.08%	34.92%
Canada	90.00%	10.00%

Table 6.80: **Percentage of libraries where Circulation Department handles any part of ILL/DD/EDD, Broken Out by FTE Enrollment**

FTE Enrollment	Yes	No
Under 2,000	71.43%	28.57%
2,000-5,000	68.42%	31.58%
5,000+-15,000	62.50%	37.50%
Over 15,000	70.59%	29.41%

Has the use of ILL automation changed over the last five years? Please explain, and describe the effect it has had on workflows and staffing.

1. Yes, we use programs to help with workflow such as Clio and Odyssey.

2. No automated processes are used.

3. Yes. We now have a host of electronic systems such as ILLiad, ArticleReach, INN-Reach, RAPID, which handle most requests in unmediated fashion. Last year 75% of our total ILL traffic was unmediated. ILL Borrowing has assumed a few of the traditional Lending duties and is now a single ILL team. Staff for that team has been reduced by 25% over the past 2 years. Many former lending duties are now handled by Materials Management & Document Delivery, which encompasses shelving, scanning, book retrieval, book returns, etc.

4. Yes. As part of the Ontario Council of Universities we started using the VDX automated ILL system, which has recently (approx 1-2 years ago) been purchased by OCLC.

5. Access to more online ILL networks has facilitated ILL work, but because of volume, staffing has not changed.

6. Electronic delivery of articles has helped us to keep up increased requests.

7. We have had no significant automation changes since adopting ILLiad in 1999.

8. Automation has not made a dramatic change in ILL, mostly due to the restrictions of our license databases, which do not allow for electronic delivery of articles. The most significant automated change is the ways in which requests are made to our ILL department - online, email, through GODOT, our link resolver. We also use technology to keep better track of our stats. These changes have not increased or decreased the number of staff in the department. Workflow is also unchanged: ILL clerk processes requests and renewals, and Circ ensure material is picked up by patron.

9. We started using prescribed software. Now there is less paperwork, staff time spent on each request is cut in half, and it is easier to keep statistics.

10. Yes, ILL/DD software system implemented, which streamlined both lending and borrowing workflows for ILL staffers.

11. Workflows have been simplified. Paperwork has been reduced. We are a small library with a very small staff. We recently replaced our interlibrary loan clerk with a library technician who has responsibilities beyond interlibrary loan.

12. Automation (new ILS, electronic delivery) has impacted us in a positive way. Patrons are more satisfied because of electronic delivery and student workers can do more work in the allotted time they're scheduled.

13. No. Our last major automation initiative related to ILL was the adoption of ILLiad in 1999.

14. We are able to process articles faster and through the use of student assistants. Tracking of delivery makes the process smoother and lending happens in a process rather than a random person-to-person performance.

15. Significantly attempting to reduce paper and automate requesting features for library patrons. In addition, the department employs much more electronic communications (email, auto generated notices) to communicate issues/problems with patrons.

16. Yes, it has changed dramatically over the past five years. Majority of our documents are sent and received electronically, thereby streamlining staff, reduction in paper usage, toner and time.

17. We have added Arial, upgraded our scanner and switched to a new library system, including ILL system. This has increased the productivity of the ILL staff and has allowed us to complete requests faster.

18. Purchase new automated ILL system. It is not steady and staff must check the daily work to see if the work was processed successfully.

19. Yes. Brief records for borrowed books/videos/CDs/DVDs/etc. are entered into the OPAC. More work for ILL librarian to enter records.

20. Electronic delivery of articles either by Ariel or email has greatly improved the turnaround time. In the next year, our library will have an ILL management system (Relais), which will have a huge impact on workflows. As yet, I cannot predict specifics, but am confident that there will be an impact.

21. Delivery systems such as ARIEL have made it easier on staff and provided speedier delivery. More pressure on infolit trainers to teach how to request ILL.

22. We have become more automated in how we deliver articles to our patrons. We now use Post to Web. So far it has not had an effect on our staffing.

23. Yes. We are now using ILLiad, which made it possible to handle increased demand without adding staff.

24. Yes. Contact is easier and faster with the use of email to ILL departments for follow-up, etc.

25. Yes. Right now ILL is very short staffed. Only one staff person is working along with a couple of student workers when available.

26. We obtained ILLiad software and this has had a huge impact. We did see increases in borrowing. It made processing materials easier, when they arrived, so workflow there eased up. Staffing has gone up in the last year or so due to increased lending.

27. None here.

28. We now use article linker to allow users to export citations to web request forms. We purchased a high-end scanner with document clean-up.

29. Not applicable. I have been here only for two years.

30. Electronic delivery. Direct request from WorldCat and databases (when fulltext not provided).

31. More automation requires the staff to be more informed about the ILL management system, circulation system and acquisitions. Staffing remains the same. The time saved in actual ILL function is used in troubleshooting technical issues with the systems being used.

32. Yes, we have moved from a paper system to the use of the ILS ILL system. We also began electronic delivery to end-user.

33. Because of the lack of support from our IT dept., our automation has actually taken a step backwards. Very frustrating. We do not offer any automated delivery (unless Faxing is considered automated!). At one time we had scanning capabilities with Ariel. Staffing has remained one full-time person.

34. No.

35. Not really but we hope to change it within the next year and it will probably increase with staffing becoming an issue.

36. Yes, using the state consortium for book delivery improved process through direct, patron-initiated borrowing.

37. Yes, we have added more patron-initiated services. Our numbers have increased and we have added staff.

38. We have added Illiad and Odyssey.

39. We use OCLC WRS and our state ILL system and have for more than 5 years. Workflows and staffing have remained the same.

40. ILLiad ILL management system implemented, enabling the unit to become more efficient. Office staff has been reduced by 1.5 FTE and activity has increased, turnaround time has been reduced, record-keeping reduced, Invoicing and payments have been reduced significantly. The unit has become more decentralized with the integration of the unit into the technical services operation. Retrieval of materials for lending has been integrated into our consortia resource sharing operation, which is defined and handled by the circulation department and bill paying integrated into the OCLC billing process handled through the administrative offices or technical services operations.

41. There is less paperwork involved. Staffing has increased due to heavier workload. It is easier to keep statistics.

42. We introduced Clio into our workflow in June 2007. This introduction has allowed us to tabulate statistics faster as well as to handle the increase in # of requests received as all requests can be routed through ClioRequests. During this same time period we also implemented Pre-populated ILL forms that have helped fill items faster and with greater accuracy. Future enhancements, such as ClioAdvanced and ILLiad, are being examined.

43. The automation of ILL has allowed staff to process ILLs faster and locate resources more accurately.

44. WorldCat resource sharing makes things so much easier. Searching is done through WorldCat and a template is created.

45. Our programs have changed along with new computers. Our staff has shrunk while the workload has grown.

46. The software for ILL is constantly being improved - OCLC and ILLiad being cases in point. Faxing is almost obsolete and scanning/emailing of materials has replaced it. Both of these have allowed more work or the same amount of work to be done by less staff.

47. Automation has reduced staffing (36 hours of student assistant work to 6 hours) and increased efficiency.

48. Not in last five years.

49. No. We have had ILLiad since 1999. At the time of installation we did see an increase in the number of requests submitted. However, the installation of ILLiad coincided with the college bringing up a new Physical Therapy Program. The library did some collection development in this area, but it was not enough. Thus, the initial 'newness' of ILLiad and the new PT program drove ILL business up quite a bit.

50. We use the software provided by our statewide consortium. Workflow has increased, staff has decreased. We are down to me (director) and my secretary.

51. Yes, increased usage of automation along with more efficient use of staff.

52. Moved to ILLiad three years ago - major effect on workflow and resulted in increased usage being handled easily by same amount of staff.

53. Staffing has decreased.25% due to ILLiad.

54. Automation has been introduced in the last five years; staffing has remained the same. Processing time has decreased.

55. Increased workflow accommodated by increased technology. Higher Technical Skills needed by Staff, training for staff greatly needed.

56. No.

57. Yes. Automation has made it easier to share the documents with other staff members. It is easily stored. System has become efficient and faster with electronic PDF formats.

58. Yes. We are currently switching from OCLC Resource Sharing to ILLiad. We want our patrons to be able to complete everything online and eliminate the need for any paper trails.

59. Yes - OCLC improved & streamlined their services. Improved time required to place and fill requests with automatic label & book band programs.

60. It is a big time saver! Has allowed us to combine Circ, reserves and ILL into one unit.

61. With Periodical Articles, the use of the Ariel system has improved the rate of delivery.

62. Yes. We now use EDD. Staffing and workflow have not changed.

63. We have the same software as five years ago: ILLiad and Ariel. Both streamline our workflow magnificently.

64. With only 18 months at the college, it is difficult to accurately answer this question. Staff size has been reduced through budget cuts/unreplaced retirements. Anecdotal evidence suggests that service has not been adversely affected.

65. No.

66. ILLiad was installed prior to five years ago. That was the biggest change in workflow - staffing has not changed for 20+ years.

67. It is now easier to produce the lists of ILL from our local ILS system.

68. Ease of use of OCLC has increased and made record-keeping much easier.

69. ILL automation software (e.g., ILLiad and OCLC Resource Sharing) has made a huge difference in the accuracy of our ILLs, with the ability to add notes and follow up on "not receiveds," and in general to provide ILL service much faster. It's streamlined our workflow, so I have more time to connect with patrons and other libraries on overdues, "not receiveds," renewal denials and subsequent 2nd copy requests. I have very little overtime now, and we've reduced our student workers from 8-9 to 6, and may reduce the staff by 1 due to attrition.

70. Implementation of ILLiad has increased efficiency and decreased workload.

Chapter Seven: Systems

Table 7.1: Percentage of libraries' ILL/DD/EDD operations that use the automated system OCLC ILLiad

	Yes	No
Entire Sample	39.76%	60.24%

Table 7.2: Percentage of libraries' ILL/DD/EDD operations that use the automated system OCLC ILLiad, Broken Out by Public or Private College

Public or Private	Yes	No
Public	42.59%	57.41%
Private	34.48%	65.52%

Table 7.3: Percentage of libraries' ILL/DD/EDD operations that use the automated system OCLC ILLiad, Broken Out by Type of College

Type of College	Yes	No
Community College	9.09%	90.91%
4-Year or M.A. Level	35.29%	64.71%
Ph.D. Level	50.00%	50.00%
Research University	66.67%	33.33%

Table 7.4: Percentage of libraries' ILL/DD/EDD operations that use the automated system OCLC ILLiad, Broken Out by Country

Country	Yes	No
U.S.A.	43.66%	56.34%
Canada	18.18%	81.82%

Table 7.5: Percentage of libraries' ILL/DD/EDD operations that use the automated system OCLC ILLiad, Broken Out by FTE Enrollment

FTE Enrollment	Yes	No
Under 2,000	18.75%	81.25%
2,000-5,000	36.36%	63.64%
5,000+-15,000	56.00%	44.00%
Over 15,000	40.00%	60.00%

Table 7.6: Percentage of libraries' ILL/DD/EDD operations that use the automated system OCLC ILL Subsystem

	Yes	No
Entire Sample	37.35%	62.65%

Table 7.7:   Percentage of libraries' ILL/DD/EDD operations that use the automated system OCLC ILL Subsystem, Broken Out by Public or Private College

Public or Private	Yes	No
Public	40.74%	59.26%
Private	31.03%	68.97%

Table 7.8:   Percentage of libraries' ILL/DD/EDD operations that use the automated system OCLC ILL Subsystem, Broken Out by Type of College

Type of College	Yes	No
Community College	54.55%	45.45%
4-Year or M.A. Level	29.41%	70.59%
Ph.D. Level	34.62%	65.38%
Research University	27.78%	72.22%

Table 7.9:   Percentage of libraries' ILL/DD/EDD operations that use the automated system OCLC ILL Subsystem, Broken Out by Country

Country	Yes	No
U.S.A.	39.44%	60.56%
Canada	27.27%	72.73%

Table 7.10:   Percentage of libraries' ILL/DD/EDD operations that use the automated system OCLC ILL Subsystem, Broken Out by FTE Enrollment

FTE Enrollment	Yes	No
Under 2,000	31.25%	68.75%
2,000-5,000	40.91%	59.09%
5,000+-15,000	36.00%	64.00%
Over 15,000	40.00%	60.00%

Table 7.11:   Percentage of libraries' ILL/DD/EDD operations that use the automated system OCLC Odyssey

	Yes	No
Entire Sample	33.73%	66.27%

Table 7.12:   Percentage of libraries' ILL/DD/EDD operations that use the automated system OCLC Odyssey, Broken Out by Public or Private College

Public or Private	Yes	No
Public	35.19%	64.81%
Private	31.03%	68.97%

Table 7.13:   Percentage of libraries' ILL/DD/EDD operations that use the automated system OCLC Odyssey, Broken Out by Type of College

Type of College	Yes	No
Community College	4.55%	95.45%
4-Year or M.A. Level	35.29%	64.71%
Ph.D. Level	46.15%	53.85%
Research University	50.00%	50.00%

Table 7.14:   Percentage of libraries' ILL/DD/EDD operations that use the automated system OCLC Odyssey, Broken Out by Country

Country	Yes	No
U.S.A.	39.44%	60.56%
Canada	0.00%	100.00%

Table 7.15:   Percentage of libraries' ILL/DD/EDD operations that use the automated system OCLC Odyssey, Broken Out by FTE Enrollment

FTE Enrollment	Yes	No
Under 2,000	31.25%	68.75%
2,000-5,000	22.73%	77.27%
5,000+-15,000	44.00%	56.00%
Over 15,000	35.00%	65.00%

Table 7.16:   Percentage of libraries' ILL/DD/EDD operations that use the automated system Ariel

	Yes	No
Entire Sample	55.42%	44.58%

Table 7.17:   Percentage of libraries' ILL/DD/EDD operations that use the automated system Ariel, Broken Out by Public or Private College

Public or Private	Yes	No
Public	51.85%	48.15%
Private	62.07%	37.93%

Table 7.18:   Percentage of libraries' ILL/DD/EDD operations that use the automated system Ariel, Broken Out by Type of College

Type of College	Yes	No
Community College	22.73%	77.27%
4-Year or M.A. Level	52.94%	47.06%
Ph.D. Level	76.92%	23.08%
Research University	66.67%	33.33%

Table 7.19:   Percentage of libraries' ILL/DD/EDD operations that use the automated system Ariel, Broken Out by Country

Country	Yes	No
U.S.A.	52.11%	47.89%
Canada	72.73%	27.27%

Table 7.20:   Percentage of libraries' ILL/DD/EDD operations that use the automated system Ariel, Broken Out by FTE Enrollment

FTE Enrollment	Yes	No
Under 2,000	43.75%	56.25%
2,000-5,000	40.91%	59.09%
5,000+-15,000	80.00%	20.00%
Over 15,000	50.00%	50.00%

Table 7.21:   Percentage of libraries' ILL/DD/EDD operations that use the automated system DOCLINE

	Yes	No
Entire Sample	10.84%	89.16%

Table 7.22:   Percentage of libraries' ILL/DD/EDD operations that use the automated system DOCLINE, Broken Out by Public or Private College

Public or Private	Yes	No
Public	9.26%	90.74%
Private	13.79%	86.21%

Table 7.23:   Percentage of libraries' ILL/DD/EDD operations that use the automated system DOCLINE, Broken Out by Type of College

Type of College	Yes	No
Community College	9.09%	90.91%
4-Year or M.A. Level	11.76%	88.24%
Ph.D. Level	7.69%	92.31%
Research University	16.67%	83.33%

Table 7.24:   Percentage of libraries' ILL/DD/EDD operations that use the automated system DOCLINE, Broken Out by Country

Country	Yes	No
U.S.A.	12.68%	87.32%
Canada	0.00%	100.00%

Table 7.25: Percentage of libraries' ILL/DD/EDD operations that use the automated system DOCLINE, Broken Out by FTE Enrollment

FTE Enrollment	Yes	No
Under 2,000	0.00%	100.00%
2,000-5,000	18.18%	81.82%
5,000+-15,000	12.00%	88.00%
Over 15,000	10.00%	90.00%

Table 7.26: Percentage of libraries' ILL/DD/EDD operations that use the automated system WorldCat Local

	Yes	No
Entire Sample	21.69%	78.31%

Table 7.27: Percentage of libraries' ILL/DD/EDD operations that use the automated system WorldCat Local, Broken Out by Public or Private College

Public or Private	Yes	No
Public	24.07%	75.93%
Private	17.24%	82.76%

Table 7.28: Percentage of libraries' ILL/DD/EDD operations that use the automated system WorldCat Local, Broken Out by Type of College

Type of College	Yes	No
Community College	27.27%	72.73%
4-Year or M.A. Level	17.65%	82.35%
Ph.D. Level	26.92%	73.08%
Research University	11.11%	88.89%

Table 7.29: Percentage of libraries' ILL/DD/EDD operations that use the automated system WorldCat Local, Broken Out by Country

Country	Yes	No
U.S.A.	22.54%	77.46%
Canada	9.09%	90.91%

Table 7.30: Percentage of libraries' ILL/DD/EDD operations that use the automated system WorldCat Local, Broken Out by FTE Enrollment

FTE Enrollment	Yes	No
Under 2,000	18.75%	81.25%
2,000-5,000	18.18%	81.82%
5,000+-15,000	24.00%	76.00%
Over 15,000	25.00%	75.00%

Table 7.31: **Percentage of libraries' ILL/DD/EDD operations that use Link Resolvers**

	Yes	No
Entire Sample	22.89%	77.11%

Table 7.32: **Percentage of libraries' ILL/DD/EDD operations that use Link Resolvers, Broken Out by Public or Private College**

Public or Private	Yes	No
Public	22.22%	77.78%
Private	24.14%	75.86%

Table 7.33: **Percentage of libraries' ILL/DD/EDD operations that use Link Resolvers, Broken Out by Type of College**

Type of College	Yes	No
Community College	22.73%	77.27%
4-Year or M.A. Level	17.65%	82.35%
Ph.D. Level	26.92%	73.08%
Research University	22.22%	77.78%

Table 7.34: **Percentage of libraries' ILL/DD/EDD operations that use Link Resolvers, Broken Out by Country**

Country	Yes	No
U.S.A.	19.72%	80.28%
Canada	45.45%	54.55%

Table 7.35: **Percentage of libraries' ILL/DD/EDD operations that use Link Resolvers, Broken Out by FTE Enrollment**

FTE Enrollment	Yes	No
Under 2,000	18.75%	81.25%
2,000-5,000	22.73%	77.27%
5,000+-15,000	24.00%	76.00%
Over 15,000	25.00%	75.00%

Table 7.36: **Percentage of libraries' ILL/DD/EDD operations that use the automated system OCLC E-Serial Holdings**

	Yes	No
Entire Sample	6.10%	93.90%

Table 7.37:   Percentage of libraries' ILL/DD/EDD operations that use the automated system OCLC E-Serial Holdings, Broken Out by Public or Private College

Public or Private	Yes	No
Public	5.56%	94.44%
Private	7.14%	92.86%

Table 7.38:   Percentage of libraries' ILL/DD/EDD operations that use the automated system OCLC E-Serial Holdings, Broken Out by Type of College

Type of College	Yes	No
Community College	0.00%	100.00%
4-Year or M.A. Level	6.25%	93.75%
Ph.D. Level	7.69%	92.31%
Research University	11.11%	88.89%

Table 7.39:   Percentage of libraries' ILL/DD/EDD operations that use the automated system OCLC E-Serial Holdings, Broken Out by Country

Country	Yes	No
U.S.A.	7.14%	92.86%
Canada	0.00%	100.00%

Table 7.40:   Percentage of libraries' ILL/DD/EDD operations that use the automated system OCLC E-Serial Holdings, Broken Out by FTE Enrollment

FTE Enrollment	Yes	No
Under 2,000	6.67%	93.33%
2,000-5,000	4.55%	95.45%
5,000+-15,000	8.00%	92.00%
Over 15,000	5.00%	95.00%

Table 7.41:   Percentage of libraries for which Digital Rights Management Control Technologies Employed by Publishers or Hardware Manufacturers have affected the ability to utilize electronic articles or e-reserves, digital copying, digital document delivery or interlibrary loan

	Yes	No
Entire Sample	41.67%	58.33%

Table 7.42:   Percentage of libraries for which Digital Rights Management Control Technologies Employed by Publishers or Hardware Manufacturers have affected the ability to utilize electronic articles or e-reserves, digital copying, digital document delivery or interlibrary loan, Broken Out by Public or Private College

Public or Private	Yes	No
Public	45.65%	54.35%
Private	34.62%	65.38%

Table 7.43: Percentage of libraries for which Digital Rights Management Control Technologies Employed by Publishers or Hardware Manufacturers have affected the ability to utilize electronic articles or e-reserves, digital copying, digital document delivery or interlibrary loan, Broken Out by Type of College

Type of College	Yes	No
Community College	33.33%	66.67%
4-Year or M.A. Level	20.00%	80.00%
Ph.D. Level	56.52%	43.48%
Research University	53.85%	46.15%

Table 7.44: Percentage of libraries for which Digital Rights Management Control Technologies Employed by Publishers or Hardware Manufacturers have affected the ability to utilize electronic articles or e-reserves, digital copying, digital document delivery or interlibrary loan, Broken Out by Country

Country	Yes	No
U.S.A.	37.70%	62.30%
Canada	70.00%	30.00%

Table 7.45: Percentage of libraries for which Digital Rights Management Control Technologies Employed by Publishers or Hardware Manufacturers have affected the ability to utilize electronic articles or e-reserves, digital copying, digital document delivery or interlibrary loan, Broken Out by FTE Enrollment

FTE Enrollment	Yes	No
Under 2,000	21.43%	78.57%
2,000-5,000	27.78%	72.22%
5,000+-15,000	52.17%	47.83%
Over 15,000	58.82%	41.18%

Table 7.46: Percentage of libraries that have ever tried to negotiate broader license terms for institutional and patron use of their digital collections, specifically for interlibrary loan and e-reserve use

	Yes	No
Entire Sample	20.00%	80.00%

Table 7.47: Percentage of libraries that have ever tried to negotiate broader license terms for institutional and patron use of their digital collections, specifically for interlibrary loan and e-reserve use, Broken Out by Public or Private College

Public or Private	Yes	No
Public	22.22%	77.78%
Private	16.00%	84.00%

Table 7.48: Percentage of libraries that have ever tried to negotiate broader license terms for institutional and patron use of their digital collections, specifically for interlibrary loan and e-reserve use, Broken Out by Type of College

Type of College	Yes	No
Community College	4.55%	95.45%
4-Year or M.A. Level	13.33%	86.67%
Ph.D. Level	31.82%	68.18%
Research University	36.36%	63.64%

Table 7.49: Percentage of libraries that have ever tried to negotiate broader license terms for institutional and patron use of their digital collections, specifically for interlibrary loan and e-reserve use, Broken Out by Country

Country	Yes	No
U.S.A.	19.67%	80.33%
Canada	25.00%	75.00%

Table 7.50: Percentage of libraries that have ever tried to negotiate broader license terms for institutional and patron use of their digital collections, specifically for interlibrary loan and e-reserve use, Broken Out by FTE Enrollment

FTE Enrollment	Yes	No
Under 2,000	14.29%	85.71%
2,000-5,000	5.88%	94.12%
5,000+-15,000	31.82%	68.18%
Over 15,000	23.53%	76.47%

If your library has made such efforts, about what percentage of the time has your library been able to alter in any way the terms of interlibrary loan so that they are in your view more favorable for the library?

1. Most of the time.

2. Person responsible was unavailable at time of survey.

3. 75%

4. N/A; our licenses are largely negotiated by the governing body of our consortium, of which we are a member.

5. N/A

6. Don't understand the wording of the question, so it's impossible to give an intelligent answer.

7. N/A

8. Unsure of percentage, but almost all of our licenses offer ILL rights.

9. N/A

10. N/A

11. More than 90%.

12. Info not available to me. Contract negotiations are handled by another staff member who does not respond to my requests for information.

13. 75%

14. Not responsible for this area - no number.

15. N/A

16. N/A

17. Unknown

18. N/A

19. N/A

20. Handled by our main branch, I do not know the answer to this question.

21. N/A

22. 10%

23. N/A

24. 75%

25. N/A

26. N/A

27. We have always negotiated licenses that are favorable to Interlibrary Loan.

28. N/A

29. 90%

Table 7.51:   Percentage of libraries that report turnaround time in their ILL statistics

	Yes	No
Entire Sample	47.06%	52.94%

Table 7.52: Percentage of libraries that report turnaround time in their ILL statistics, Broken Out by Public or Private College

Public or Private	Yes	No
Public	51.85%	48.15%
Private	38.71%	61.29%

Table 7.53: Percentage of libraries that report turnaround time in their ILL statistics, Broken Out by Type of College

Type of College	Yes	No
Community College	45.45%	54.55%
4-Year or M.A. Level	47.06%	52.94%
Ph.D. Level	53.57%	46.43%
Research University	38.89%	61.11%

Table 7.54: Percentage of libraries that report turnaround time in their ILL statistics, Broken Out by Country

Country	Yes	No
U.S.A.	47.95%	52.05%
Canada	36.36%	63.64%

Table 7.55: Percentage of libraries that report turnaround time in their ILL statistics, Broken Out by FTE Enrollment

FTE Enrollment	Yes	No
Under 2,000	37.50%	62.50%
2,000-5,000	43.48%	56.52%
5,000+-15,000	61.54%	38.46%
Over 15,000	40.00%	60.00%

Table 7.56: Percentage of libraries that report who borrowed from whom in their ILL statistics

	Yes	No
Entire Sample	43.53%	56.47%

Table 7.57: Percentage of libraries that report who borrowed from whom in their ILL statistics, Broken Out by Public or Private College

Public or Private	Yes	No
Public	50.00%	50.00%
Private	32.26%	67.74%

Table 7.58: Percentage of libraries that report who borrowed from whom in their ILL statistics, Broken Out by Type of College

Type of College	Yes	No
Community College	59.09%	40.91%
4-Year or M.A. Level	35.29%	64.71%
Ph.D. Level	35.71%	64.29%
Research University	44.44%	55.56%

Table 7.59: Percentage of libraries that report who borrowed from whom in their ILL statistics, Broken Out by Country

Country	Yes	No
U.S.A.	41.10%	58.90%
Canada	54.55%	45.45%

Table 7.60: Percentage of libraries that report who borrowed from whom in their ILL statistics, Broken Out by FTE Enrollment

FTE Enrollment	Yes	No
Under 2,000	31.25%	68.75%
2,000-5,000	30.43%	69.57%
5,000+-15,000	57.69%	42.31%
Over 15,000	50.00%	50.00%

Table 7.61: Percentage of libraries that report most requested books and journals in their ILL statistics

	Yes	No
Entire Sample	34.12%	65.88%

Table 7.62: Percentage of libraries that report most requested books and journals in their ILL statistics, Broken Out by Public or Private College

Public or Private	Yes	No
Public	38.89%	61.11%
Private	25.81%	74.19%

Table 7.63: Percentage of libraries that report most requested books and journals in their ILL statistics, Broken Out by Type of College

Type of College	Yes	No
Community College	22.73%	77.27%
4-Year or M.A. Level	23.53%	76.47%
Ph.D. Level	42.86%	57.14%
Research University	44.44%	55.56%

Table 7.64: **Percentage of libraries that report most requested books and journals in their ILL statistics, Broken Out by Country**

Country	Yes	No
U.S.A.	36.99%	63.01%
Canada	18.18%	81.82%

Table 7.65: **Percentage of libraries that report most requested books and journals in their ILL statistics, Broken Out by FTE Enrollment**

FTE Enrollment	Yes	No
Under 2,000	18.75%	81.25%
2,000-5,000	21.74%	78.26%
5,000+-15,000	53.85%	46.15%
Over 15,000	35.00%	65.00%

Table 7.66: **Percentage of libraries that report number lent in their ILL statistics**

	Yes	No
Entire Sample	84.71%	15.29%

Table 7.67: **Percentage of libraries that report number lent in their ILL statistics, Broken Out by Public or Private College**

Public or Private	Yes	No
Public	87.04%	12.96%
Private	80.65%	19.35%

Table 7.68: **Percentage of libraries that report number lent in their ILL statistics, Broken Out by Type of College**

Type of College	Yes	No
Community College	100.00%	0.00%
4-Year or M.A. Level	88.24%	11.76%
Ph.D. Level	78.57%	21.43%
Research University	72.22%	27.78%

Table 7.69: **Percentage of libraries that report number lent in their ILL statistics, Broken Out by Country**

Country	Yes	No
U.S.A.	84.93%	15.07%
Canada	90.91%	9.09%

Table 7.70:   Percentage of libraries that report number lent in their ILL statistics, Broken Out by FTE Enrollment

FTE Enrollment	Yes	No
Under 2,000	87.50%	12.50%
2,000-5,000	78.26%	21.74%
5,000+-15,000	88.46%	11.54%
Over 15,000	85.00%	15.00%

Table 7.71:   Percentage of libraries that report number borrowed and filled in their ILL statistics

	Yes	No
Entire Sample	84.71%	15.29%

Table 7.72:   Percentage of libraries that report number borrowed and filled in their ILL statistics, Broken Out by Public or Private College

Public or Private	Yes	No
Public	87.04%	12.96%
Private	80.65%	19.35%

Table 7.73:   Percentage of libraries that report number borrowed and filled in their ILL statistics, Broken Out by Type of College

Type of College	Yes	No
Community College	100.00%	0.00%
4-Year or M.A. Level	82.35%	17.65%
Ph.D. Level	82.14%	17.86%
Research University	72.22%	27.78%

Table 7.74:   Percentage of libraries that report number borrowed and filled in their ILL statistics, Broken Out by Country

Country	Yes	No
U.S.A.	83.56%	16.44%
Canada	90.91%	9.09%

Table 7.75:   Percentage of libraries that report number borrowed and filled in their ILL statistics, Broken Out by FTE Enrollment

FTE Enrollment	Yes	No
Under 2,000	81.25%	18.75%
2,000-5,000	78.26%	21.74%
5,000+-15,000	92.31%	7.69%
Over 15,000	85.00%	15.00%

Table 7.76: Percentage of libraries that report number requested and unfilled in their ILL statistics

	Yes	No
Entire Sample	74.12%	25.88%

Table 7.77: Percentage of libraries that report number requested and unfilled in their ILL statistics, Broken Out by Public or Private College

Public or Private	Yes	No
Public	81.48%	18.52%
Private	61.29%	38.71%

Table 7.78: Percentage of libraries that report number requested and unfilled in their ILL statistics, Broken Out by Type of College

Type of College	Yes	No
Community College	81.82%	18.18%
4-Year or M.A. Level	58.82%	41.18%
Ph.D. Level	78.57%	21.43%
Research University	72.22%	27.78%

Table 7.79: Percentage of libraries that report number requested and unfilled in their ILL statistics, Broken Out by Country

Country	Yes	No
U.S.A.	73.97%	26.03%
Canada	72.73%	27.27%

Table 7.80: Percentage of libraries that report number requested and unfilled in their ILL statistics, Broken Out by FTE Enrollment

FTE Enrollment	Yes	No
Under 2,000	56.25%	43.75%
2,000-5,000	65.22%	34.78%
5,000+-15,000	88.46%	11.54%
Over 15,000	80.00%	20.00%

Table 7.81: Percentage of libraries that report photocopies in their ILL statistics

	Yes	No
Entire Sample	61.18%	38.82%

Table 7.82: Percentage of libraries that report photocopies in their ILL statistics, Broken Out by Public or Private College

Public or Private	Yes	No
Public	59.26%	40.74%
Private	64.52%	35.48%

Table 7.83:   Percentage of libraries that report photocopies in their ILL statistics, Broken Out by Type of College

Type of College	Yes	No
Community College	54.55%	45.45%
4-Year or M.A. Level	64.71%	35.29%
Ph.D. Level	64.29%	35.71%
Research University	61.11%	38.89%

Table 7.84:   Percentage of libraries that report photocopies in their ILL statistics, Broken Out by Country

Country	Yes	No
U.S.A.	60.27%	39.73%
Canada	63.64%	36.36%

Table 7.85:   Percentage of libraries that report photocopies in their ILL statistics, Broken Out by FTE Enrollment

FTE Enrollment	Yes	No
Under 2,000	56.25%	43.75%
2,000-5,000	56.52%	43.48%
5,000+-15,000	69.23%	30.77%
Over 15,000	60.00%	40.00%

Table 7.86:   Percentage of libraries that report returnables in their ILL statistics

	Yes	No
Entire Sample	67.06%	32.94%

Table 7.87:   Percentage of libraries that report returnables in their ILL statistics, Broken Out by Public or Private College

Public or Private	Yes	No
Public	66.67%	33.33%
Private	67.74%	32.26%

Table 7.88:   Percentage of libraries that report returnables in their ILL statistics, Broken Out by Type of College

Type of College	Yes	No
Community College	54.55%	45.45%
4-Year or M.A. Level	64.71%	35.29%
Ph.D. Level	75.00%	25.00%
Research University	72.22%	27.78%

Table 7.89: Percentage of libraries that report returnables in their ILL statistics, Broken Out by Country

Country	Yes	No
U.S.A.	64.38%	35.62%
Canada	81.82%	18.18%

Table 7.90: Percentage of libraries that report returnables in their ILL statistics, Broken Out by FTE Enrollment

FTE Enrollment	Yes	No
Under 2,000	56.25%	43.75%
2,000-5,000	60.87%	39.13%
5,000+-15,000	84.62%	15.38%
Over 15,000	60.00%	40.00%

Table 7.91: Percentage of libraries that report non-returnables in their ILL statistics

	Yes	No
Entire Sample	51.76%	48.24%

Table 7.92: Percentage of libraries that report non-returnables in their ILL statistics, Broken Out by Public or Private College

Public or Private	Yes	No
Public	53.70%	46.30%
Private	48.39%	51.61%

Table 7.93: Percentage of libraries that report non-returnables in their ILL statistics, Broken Out by Type of College

Type of College	Yes	No
Community College	40.91%	59.09%
4-Year or M.A. Level	47.06%	52.94%
Ph.D. Level	53.57%	46.43%
Research University	66.67%	33.33%

Table 7.94: Percentage of libraries that report non-returnables in their ILL statistics, Broken Out by Country

Country	Yes	No
U.S.A.	50.68%	49.32%
Canada	63.64%	36.36%

Table 7.95: Percentage of libraries that report non-returnables in their ILL statistics, Broken Out by FTE Enrollment

FTE Enrollment	Yes	No
Under 2,000	37.50%	62.50%
2,000-5,000	52.17%	47.83%
5,000+-15,000	57.69%	42.31%
Over 15,000	55.00%	45.00%

Table 7.96: Percentage of libraries that report in-state loans in their ILL statistics

	Yes	No
Entire Sample	40.00%	60.00%

Table 7.97: Percentage of libraries that report in-state loans in their ILL statistics, Broken Out by Public or Private College

Public or Private	Yes	No
Public	40.74%	59.26%
Private	38.71%	61.29%

Table 7.98: Percentage of libraries that report in-state loans in their ILL statistics, Broken Out by Type of College

Type of College	Yes	No
Community College	59.09%	40.91%
4-Year or M.A. Level	47.06%	52.94%
Ph.D. Level	25.00%	75.00%
Research University	33.33%	66.67%

Table 7.99: Percentage of libraries that report in-state loans in their ILL statistics, Broken Out by Country

Country	Yes	No
U.S.A.	41.10%	58.90%
Canada	36.36%	63.64%

Table 7.100: Percentage of libraries that report in-state loans in their ILL statistics, Broken Out by FTE Enrollment

FTE Enrollment	Yes	No
Under 2,000	37.50%	62.50%
2,000-5,000	26.09%	73.91%
5,000+-15,000	53.85%	46.15%
Over 15,000	40.00%	60.00%

Table 7.101: Percentage of libraries that report out-of-state loans in their ILL statistics

	Yes	No
Entire Sample	36.47%	63.53%

Table 7.102: Percentage of libraries that report out-of-state loans in their ILL statistics, Broken Out by Public or Private College

Public or Private	Yes	No
Public	37.04%	62.96%
Private	35.48%	64.52%

Table 7.103: Percentage of libraries that report out-of-state loans in their ILL statistics, Broken Out by Type of College

Type of College	Yes	No
Community College	54.55%	45.45%
4-Year or M.A. Level	41.18%	58.82%
Ph.D. Level	25.00%	75.00%
Research University	27.78%	72.22%

Table 7.104: Percentage of libraries that report out-of-state loans in their ILL statistics, Broken Out by Country

Country	Yes	No
U.S.A.	36.99%	63.01%
Canada	36.36%	63.64%

Table 7.105: Percentage of libraries that report out-of-state loans in their ILL statistics, Broken Out by FTE Enrollment

FTE Enrollment	Yes	No
Under 2,000	31.25%	68.75%
2,000-5,000	26.09%	73.91%
5,000+-15,000	46.15%	53.85%
Over 15,000	40.00%	60.00%

Table 7.106: Percentage of libraries that report international loans in their ILL statistics

	Yes	No
Entire Sample	11.76%	88.24%

Table 7.107: Percentage of libraries that report international loans in their ILL statistics, Broken Out by Public or Private College

Public or Private	Yes	No
Public	14.81%	85.19%
Private	6.45%	93.55%

Table 7.108: Percentage of libraries that report international loans in their ILL statistics, Broken Out by Type of College

Type of College	Yes	No
Community College	13.64%	86.36%
4-Year or M.A. Level	5.88%	94.12%
Ph.D. Level	10.71%	89.29%
Research University	16.67%	83.33%

Table 7.109: Percentage of libraries that report international loans in their ILL statistics, Broken Out by Country

Country	Yes	No
U.S.A.	8.22%	91.78%
Canada	36.36%	63.64%

Table 7.110: Percentage of libraries that report international loans in their ILL statistics, Broken Out by FTE Enrollment

FTE Enrollment	Yes	No
Under 2,000	0.00%	100.00%
2,000-5,000	4.35%	95.65%
5,000+-15,000	19.23%	80.77%
Over 15,000	20.00%	80.00%

Table 7.111: Percentage of libraries that report Ariel delivery in their ILL statistics

	Yes	No
Entire Sample	18.82%	81.18%

Table 7.112: Percentage of libraries that report Ariel delivery in their ILL statistics, Broken Out by Public or Private College

Public or Private	Yes	No
Public	16.67%	83.33%
Private	22.58%	77.42%

Table 7.113: Percentage of libraries that report Ariel delivery in their ILL statistics, Broken Out by Type of College

Type of College	Yes	No
Community College	13.64%	86.36%
4-Year or M.A. Level	11.76%	88.24%
Ph.D. Level	32.14%	67.86%
Research University	11.11%	88.89%

Table 7.114: Percentage of libraries that report Ariel delivery in their ILL statistics, Broken Out by Country

Country	Yes	No
U.S.A.	17.81%	82.19%
Canada	27.27%	72.73%

Table 7.115: Percentage of libraries that report Ariel delivery in their ILL statistics, Broken Out by FTE Enrollment

FTE Enrollment	Yes	No
Under 2,000	12.50%	87.50%
2,000-5,000	17.39%	82.61%
5,000+-15,000	26.92%	73.08%
Over 15,000	15.00%	85.00%

Table 7.116: Percentage of libraries that report email delivery in their ILL statistics

	Yes	No
Entire Sample	14.12%	85.88%

Table 7.117: Percentage of libraries that report email delivery in their ILL statistics, Broken Out by Public or Private College

Public or Private	Yes	No
Public	14.81%	85.19%
Private	12.90%	87.10%

Table 7.118: Percentage of libraries that report email delivery in their ILL statistics, Broken Out by Type of College

Type of College	Yes	No
Community College	9.09%	90.91%
4-Year or M.A. Level	11.76%	88.24%
Ph.D. Level	17.86%	82.14%
Research University	16.67%	83.33%

Table 7.119: Percentage of libraries that report email delivery in their ILL statistics, Broken Out by Country

Country	Yes	No
U.S.A.	15.07%	84.93%
Canada	9.09%	90.91%

Table 7.120: Percentage of libraries that report email delivery in their ILL statistics, Broken Out by FTE Enrollment

FTE Enrollment	Yes	No
Under 2,000	6.25%	93.75%
2,000-5,000	4.35%	95.65%
5,000+-15,000	26.92%	73.08%
Over 15,000	15.00%	85.00%

Table 7.121: Percentage of libraries that report Fax Use in their ILL statistics

	Yes	No
Entire Sample	15.29%	84.71%

Table 7.122: Percentage of libraries that report Fax Use in their ILL statistics, Broken Out by Public or Private College

Public or Private	Yes	No
Public	16.67%	83.33%
Private	12.90%	87.10%

Table 7.123: Percentage of libraries that report Fax Use in their ILL statistics, Broken Out by Type of College

Type of College	Yes	No
Community College	18.18%	81.82%
4-Year or M.A. Level	0.00%	100.00%
Ph.D. Level	17.86%	82.14%
Research University	22.22%	77.78%

Table 7.124: Percentage of libraries that report Fax Use in their ILL statistics, Broken Out by Country

Country	Yes	No
U.S.A.	15.07%	84.93%
Canada	18.18%	81.82%

Table 7.125: Percentage of libraries that report Fax Use in their ILL statistics, Broken Out by FTE Enrollment

FTE Enrollment	Yes	No
Under 2,000	6.25%	93.75%
2,000-5,000	13.04%	86.96%
5,000+-15,000	23.08%	76.92%
Over 15,000	15.00%	85.00%

Table 7.126: Percentage of libraries that report OCLC Illiad in their ILL statistics

	Yes	No
Entire Sample	17.65%	82.35%

Table 7.127: Percentage of libraries that report OCLC Illiad in their ILL statistics, Broken Out by Public or Private College

Public or Private	Yes	No
Public	18.52%	81.48%
Private	16.13%	83.87%

Table 7.128: Percentage of libraries that report OCLC Illiad in their ILL statistics, Broken Out by Type of College

Type of College	Yes	No
Community College	0.00%	100.00%
4-Year or M.A. Level	17.65%	82.35%
Ph.D. Level	21.43%	78.57%
Research University	33.33%	66.67%

Table 7.129: Percentage of libraries that report OCLC Illiad in their ILL statistics, Broken Out by Country

Country	Yes	No
U.S.A.	20.55%	79.45%
Canada	0.00%	100.00%

Table 7.130: Percentage of libraries that report OCLC Illiad in their ILL statistics, Broken Out by FTE Enrollment

FTE Enrollment	Yes	No
Under 2,000	12.50%	87.50%
2,000-5,000	4.35%	95.65%
5,000+-15,000	34.62%	65.38%
Over 15,000	15.00%	85.00%

Table 7.131:   Percentage of libraries that report OCLC ILL Subsystem Use in their ILL statistics

	Yes	No
Entire Sample	11.76%	88.24%

Table 7.132:   Percentage of libraries that report OCLC ILL Subsystem Use in their ILL statistics, Broken Out by Public or Private College

Public or Private	Yes	No
Public	14.81%	85.19%
Private	6.45%	93.55%

Table 7.133:   Percentage of libraries that report OCLC ILL Subsystem Use in their ILL statistics, Broken Out by Type of College

Type of College	Yes	No
Community College	13.64%	86.36%
4-Year or M.A. Level	5.88%	94.12%
Ph.D. Level	17.86%	82.14%
Research University	5.56%	94.44%

Table 7.134:   Percentage of libraries that report OCLC ILL Subsystem Use in their ILL statistics, Broken Out by Country

Country	Yes	No
U.S.A.	12.33%	87.67%
Canada	9.09%	90.91%

Table 7.135:   Percentage of libraries that report OCLC ILL Subsystem Use in their ILL statistics, Broken Out by FTE Enrollment

FTE Enrollment	Yes	No
Under 2,000	6.25%	93.75%
2,000-5,000	13.04%	86.96%
5,000+-15,000	15.38%	84.62%
Over 15,000	10.00%	90.00%

Table 7.136:   Percentage of libraries that report U.S. Mail Use in their ILL statistics

	Yes	No
Entire Sample	11.76%	88.24%

Table 7.137: Percentage of libraries that report U.S. Mail Use in their ILL statistics, Broken Out by Public or Private College

Public or Private	Yes	No
Public	9.26%	90.74%
Private	16.13%	83.87%

Table 7.138: Percentage of libraries that report U.S. Mail Use in their ILL statistics, Broken Out by Type of College

Type of College	Yes	No
Community College	9.09%	90.91%
4-Year or M.A. Level	5.88%	94.12%
Ph.D. Level	21.43%	78.57%
Research University	5.56%	94.44%

Table 7.139: Percentage of libraries that report U.S. Mail Use in their ILL statistics, Broken Out by Country

Country	Yes	No
U.S.A.	12.33%	87.67%
Canada	9.09%	90.91%

Table 7.140: Percentage of libraries that report U.S. Mail Use in their ILL statistics, Broken Out by FTE Enrollment

FTE Enrollment	Yes	No
Under 2,000	6.25%	93.75%
2,000-5,000	17.39%	82.61%
5,000+-15,000	19.23%	80.77%
Over 15,000	0.00%	100.00%

Table 7.141: Percentage of libraries that report Use of Other Carriers in their ILL statistics

	Yes	No
Entire Sample	8.24%	91.76%

Table 7.142: Percentage of libraries that report Use of Other Carriers in their ILL statistics, Broken Out by Public or Private College

Public or Private	Yes	No
Public	9.26%	90.74%
Private	6.45%	93.55%

Table 7.143: Percentage of libraries that report Use of Other Carriers in their ILL statistics, Broken Out by Type of College

Type of College	Yes	No
Community College	4.55%	95.45%
4-Year or M.A. Level	11.76%	88.24%
Ph.D. Level	10.71%	89.29%
Research University	5.56%	94.44%

Table 7.144: Percentage of libraries that report Use of Other Carriers in their ILL statistics, Broken Out by Country

Country	Yes	No
U.S.A.	8.22%	91.78%
Canada	9.09%	90.91%

Table 7.145: Percentage of libraries that report Use of Other Carriers in their ILL statistics, Broken Out by FTE Enrollment

FTE Enrollment	Yes	No
Under 2,000	6.25%	93.75%
2,000-5,000	4.35%	95.65%
5,000+-15,000	19.23%	80.77%
Over 15,000	0.00%	100.00%

Table 7.146: Percentage of libraries that report Use of Courier Services in their ILL statistics

	Yes	No
Entire Sample	17.65%	82.35%

Table 7.147: Percentage of libraries that report Use of Courier Services in their ILL statistics, Broken Out by Public or Private College

Public or Private	Yes	No
Public	20.37%	79.63%
Private	12.90%	87.10%

Table 7.148: Percentage of libraries that report Use of Courier Services in their ILL statistics, Broken Out by Type of College

Type of College	Yes	No
Community College	31.82%	68.18%
4-Year or M.A. Level	5.88%	94.12%
Ph.D. Level	17.86%	82.14%
Research University	11.11%	88.89%

Table 7.149:   Percentage of libraries that report Use of Courier Services in their ILL statistics, Broken Out by Country

Country	Yes	No
U.S.A.	16.44%	83.56%
Canada	27.27%	72.73%

Table 7.150:   Percentage of libraries that report Use of Courier Services in their ILL statistics, Broken Out by FTE Enrollment

FTE Enrollment	Yes	No
Under 2,000	12.50%	87.50%
2,000-5,000	17.39%	82.61%
5,000+-15,000	23.08%	76.92%
Over 15,000	15.00%	85.00%

Table 7.151:   Percentage of libraries that report Use of Statewide Consortia in their ILL statistics

	Yes	No
Entire Sample	31.76%	68.24%

Table 7.152:   Percentage of libraries that report Use of Statewide Consortia in their ILL statistics, Broken Out by Public or Private College

Public or Private	Yes	No
Public	37.04%	62.96%
Private	22.58%	77.42%

Table 7.153:   Percentage of libraries that report Use of Statewide Consortia in their ILL statistics, Broken Out by Type of College

Type of College	Yes	No
Community College	31.82%	68.18%
4-Year or M.A. Level	23.53%	76.47%
Ph.D. Level	35.71%	64.29%
Research University	33.33%	66.67%

Table 7.154:   Percentage of libraries that report Use of Statewide Consortia in their ILL statistics, Broken Out by Country

Country	Yes	No
U.S.A.	30.14%	69.86%
Canada	45.45%	54.55%

Table 7.155: Percentage of libraries that report Use of Statewide Consortia in their ILL statistics, Broken Out by FTE Enrollment

FTE Enrollment	Yes	No
Under 2,000	25.00%	75.00%
2,000-5,000	17.39%	82.61%
5,000+-15,000	38.46%	61.54%
Over 15,000	45.00%	55.00%

Table 7.156: Percentage of libraries that report Use of Other Consortia/Groups in their ILL statistics

	Yes	No
Entire Sample	17.65%	82.35%

Table 7.157: Percentage of libraries that report Use of Other Consortia/Groups in their ILL statistics, Broken Out by Public or Private College

Public or Private	Yes	No
Public	18.52%	81.48%
Private	16.13%	83.87%

Table 7.158: Percentage of libraries that report Use of Other Consortia/Groups in their ILL statistics, Broken Out by Type of College

Type of College	Yes	No
Community College	9.09%	90.91%
4-Year or M.A. Level	11.76%	88.24%
Ph.D. Level	21.43%	78.57%
Research University	27.78%	72.22%

Table 7.159: Percentage of libraries that report Use of Other Consortia/Groups in their ILL statistics, Broken Out by Country

Country	Yes	No
U.S.A.	17.81%	82.19%
Canada	18.18%	81.82%

Table 7.160: Percentage of libraries that report Use of Other Consortia/Groups in their ILL statistics, Broken Out by FTE Enrollment

FTE Enrollment	Yes	No
Under 2,000	6.25%	93.75%
2,000-5,000	13.04%	86.96%
5,000+-15,000	23.08%	76.92%
Over 15,000	25.00%	75.00%

Table 7.161: Percentage of libraries that report Walk-ins in their ILL statistics

	Yes	No
Entire Sample	8.24%	91.76%

Table 7.162: Percentage of libraries that report Walk-ins in their ILL statistics, Broken Out by Public or Private College

Public or Private	Yes	No
Public	7.41%	92.59%
Private	9.68%	90.32%

Table 7.163: Percentage of libraries that report Walk-ins in their ILL statistics, Broken Out by Type of College

Type of College	Yes	No
Community College	4.55%	95.45%
4-Year or M.A. Level	5.88%	94.12%
Ph.D. Level	17.86%	82.14%
Research University	0.00%	100.00%

Table 7.164: Percentage of libraries that report Walk-ins in their ILL statistics, Broken Out by Country

Country	Yes	No
U.S.A.	6.85%	93.15%
Canada	18.18%	81.82%

Table 7.165: Percentage of libraries that report Walk-ins in their ILL statistics, Broken Out by FTE Enrollment

FTE Enrollment	Yes	No
Under 2,000	6.25%	93.75%
2,000-5,000	8.70%	91.30%
5,000+-15,000	11.54%	88.46%
Over 15,000	5.00%	95.00%

Chapter Eight: Workflow Studies

Table 8.1: Percentage of libraries whose ILL/DD/EDD unit has performed workflow studies to review practices and staffing

	Yes	No
Entire Sample	21.92%	78.08%

Table 8.2: Percentage of libraries whose ILL/DD/EDD unit has performed workflow studies to review practices and staffing, Broken Out by Public or Private College

Public or Private	Yes	No
Public	23.40%	76.60%
Private	19.23%	80.77%

Table 8.3: Percentage of libraries whose ILL/DD/EDD unit has performed workflow studies to review practices and staffing, Broken Out by Type of College

Type of College	Yes	No
Community College	9.09%	90.91%
4-Year or M.A. Level	13.33%	86.67%
Ph.D. Level	26.09%	73.91%
Research University	46.15%	53.85%

Table 8.4: Percentage of libraries whose ILL/DD/EDD unit has performed workflow studies to review practices and staffing, Broken Out by Country

Country	Yes	No
U.S.A.	14.52%	85.48%
Canada	60.00%	40.00%

Table 8.5: Percentage of libraries whose ILL/DD/EDD unit has performed workflow studies to review practices and staffing, Broken Out by FTE Enrollment

FTE Enrollment	Yes	No
Under 2,000	21.43%	78.57%
2,000-5,000	16.67%	83.33%
5,000+-15,000	25.00%	75.00%
Over 15,000	23.53%	76.47%

If the library has performed workflow studies for ILL, please describe the purposes of the studies and outline what changes resulted from them.

1. We looked at changes in workflow due to unmediated borrowing and addition of link resolver, as well as common functions performed by ILL, Reserve, shelving. This resulted in a reorganization of Access Services from "units" of ILL Borrowing, ILL Lending, Shelving, Billing, Circulation and Reserves to "teams": ILL, Materials Management & Document Delivery; Circulation; Reserve.

2. To improve turnaround time and efficiency. Resulting changes listed below. Additional use of software to reduce paper / filing. Use of circulation to improve end-user access and tracking.

3. To streamline ILL process.

4. Ongoing project. The purpose is to ensure workflow is as simple and streamlined as possible to increase turnaround time of service and to decrease unnecessary work for staff. One change so far has been to move to paperless stats and centralizing stats gathering into a single online form.

5. N/A

6. While we have not performed a formal workflow study, examination of processes and workflow is ongoing.

7. N/A

8. N/A

9. Streamlined workflows and explained the importance of workflows.

10. We did this process a number of years ago so any data would now be out of date. At that time we used to determine turnaround time at various stages in the ordering process.

11. Purposes: Training new staff; diagnosing system problems; eliminating practices.

12. Office efficiencies. Streamlining procedures.

13. N/A

14. N/A

15. The workflow study was performed approximately 5 years ago. It was used to determine the efficiency of the work space and how to better set up and maintain the ILL department. It resulted in ILL offices being moved to a different location within the library that allowed for greater space and more room to process and fill requests.

16. N/A

17. Studies were for the purpose of streamlining and resulted in best practices.

18. N/A

19. Merged services (circulation, ILL, reserves) into Reader Services with cross training and training of 24-hour staff to complete ILL/DD work.

20. Looked at use of student assistants and time.

21. Statistics provided to Director.

22. N/A

23. Too many requests were received in both borrowing and lending. Student hours were increased to help the department.

24. OCLC did one when we decided to make the change to ILLiad. We are a one-person ILL department so there wasn't much change to be made.

25. N/A

26. N/A

27. N/A

Chapter Nine: Personnel

Table 9.1: Percentage of libraries whose Interlibrary Loan or Document Delivery department requires an MLS/MLIS librarian to supervise its operations

	Yes	No
Entire Sample	39.73%	60.27%

Table 9.2: Percentage of libraries whose Interlibrary Loan or Document Delivery department requires an MLS/MLIS librarian to supervise its operations, Broken Out by Public or Private College

Public or Private	Yes	No
Public	30.61%	69.39%
Private	58.33%	41.67%

Table 9.3: Percentage of libraries whose Interlibrary Loan or Document Delivery department requires an MLS/MLIS librarian to supervise its operations, Broken Out by Type of College

Type of College	Yes	No
Community College	31.82%	68.18%
4-Year or M.A. Level	46.67%	53.33%
Ph.D. Level	54.55%	45.45%
Research University	21.43%	78.57%

Table 9.4: Percentage of libraries whose Interlibrary Loan or Document Delivery department requires an MLS/MLIS librarian to supervise its operations, Broken Out by Country

Country	Yes	No
U.S.A.	37.70%	62.30%
Canada	45.45%	54.55%

Table 9.5: Percentage of libraries whose Interlibrary Loan or Document Delivery department requires an MLS/MLIS librarian to supervise its operations, Broken Out by FTE Enrollment

FTE Enrollment	Yes	No
Under 2,000	46.67%	53.33%
2,000-5,000	38.89%	61.11%
5,000+-15,000	43.48%	56.52%
Over 15,000	29.41%	70.59%

Table 9.6: Mean, Median, Minimum and Maximum number of FTE positions in library's ILL/DD/EDD staff

	Mean	Median	Minimum	Maximum
Entire Sample	1.90	1.13	0.00	16.25

Table 9.7: Mean, Median, Minimum and Maximum number of FTE positions in library's ILL/DD/EDD staff, Broken Out by Public or Private College

Public or Private	Mean	Median	Minimum	Maximum
Public	2.03	1.38	0.00	16.25
Private	1.65	1.00	0.20	5.00

Table 9.8: Mean, Median, Minimum and Maximum number of FTE positions in library's ILL/DD/EDD staff, Broken Out by Type of College

Type of College	Mean	Median	Minimum	Maximum
Community College	1.01	1.00	0.00	2.00
4-Year or M.A. Level	1.53	1.50	0.20	2.50
Ph.D. Level	2.08	2.00	1.00	5.00
Research University	3.33	2.05	0.25	16.25

Table 9.9: Mean, Median, Minimum and Maximum number of FTE positions in library's ILL/DD/EDD staff, Broken Out by Country

Country	Mean	Median	Minimum	Maximum
U.S.A.	1.92	1.00	0.00	16.25
Canada	1.92	2.00	0.30	4.75

Table 9.10: Mean, Median, Minimum and Maximum number of FTE positions in library's ILL/DD/EDD staff, Broken Out by FTE Enrollment

FTE Enrollment	Mean	Median	Minimum	Maximum
Under 2,000	1.12	1.00	0.00	2.50
2,000-5,000	1.42	1.00	0.50	2.50
5,000+-15,000	2.29	2.05	0.75	5.00
Over 15,000	2.59	1.25	0.10	16.25

Table 9.11: Mean, Median, Minimum and Maximum number of Full-time Professionals (MLS) on library's ILL/DD/EDD staff

	Mean	Median	Minimum	Maximum
Entire Sample	0.52	0.50	0.00	2.00

Table 9.12:   Mean, Median, Minimum and Maximum number of Full-time Professionals (MLS) on library's ILL/DD/EDD staff, Broken Out by Public or Private College

Public or Private	Mean	Median	Minimum	Maximum
Public	0.37	0.00	0.00	2.00
Private	0.86	1.00	0.00	1.00

Table 9.13:   Mean, Median, Minimum and Maximum number of Full-time Professionals (MLS) on library's ILL/DD/EDD staff, Broken Out by Type of College

Type of College	Mean	Median	Minimum	Maximum
Community College	0.20	0.00	0.00	1.00
4-Year or M.A. Level	0.88	1.00	0.00	1.00
Ph.D. Level	0.71	1.00	0.00	2.00
Research University	0.22	0.00	0.00	1.00

Table 9.14:   Mean, Median, Minimum and Maximum number of Full-time Professionals (MLS) on library's ILL/DD/EDD staff, Broken Out by Country

Country	Mean	Median	Minimum	Maximum
U.S.A.	0.55	1.00	0.00	2.00
Canada	0.20	0.00	0.00	1.00

Table 9.15:   Mean, Median, Minimum and Maximum number of Full-time Professionals (MLS) on library's ILL/DD/EDD staff, Broken Out by FTE Enrollment

FTE Enrollment	Mean	Median	Minimum	Maximum
Under 2,000	0.56	1.00	0.00	1.00
2,000-5,000	0.60	1.00	0.00	1.00
5,000+-15,000	0.69	1.00	0.00	2.00
Over 15,000	0.11	0.00	0.00	1.00

Table 9.16:   Mean, Median, Minimum and Maximum number of Full-time Non-Professionals* on library's ILL/DD/EDD staff

	Mean	Median	Minimum	Maximum
Entire Sample	1.52	1.00	0.00	4.00

*Support Staff

Table 9.17:   Mean, Median, Minimum and Maximum number of Full-time Non-Professionals on library's ILL/DD/EDD staff, Broken Out by Public or Private College

Public or Private	Mean	Median	Minimum	Maximum
Public	1.59	1.00	0.00	4.00
Private	1.37	1.00	0.00	4.00

Table 9.18: Mean, Median, Minimum and Maximum number of Full-time Non-Professionals on library's ILL/DD/EDD staff, Broken Out by Type of College

Type of College	Mean	Median	Minimum	Maximum
Community College	1.00	1.00	0.00	2.00
4-Year or M.A. Level	1.00	1.00	0.00	2.00
Ph.D. Level	1.85	2.00	1.00	4.00
Research University	2.23	2.00	1.00	4.00

Table 9.19: Mean, Median, Minimum and Maximum number of Full-time Non-Professionals on library's ILL/DD/EDD staff, Broken Out by Country

Country	Mean	Median	Minimum	Maximum
U.S.A.	1.48	1.00	0.00	4.00
Canada	1.73	2.00	1.00	4.00

Table 9.20: Mean, Median, Minimum and Maximum number of Full-time Non-Professionals on library's ILL/DD/EDD staff, Broken Out by FTE Enrollment

FTE Enrollment	Mean	Median	Minimum	Maximum
Under 2,000	0.85	1.00	0.00	2.00
2,000-5,000	1.13	1.00	0.00	2.00
5,000+-15,000	2.00	2.00	1.00	4.00
Over 15,000	1.94	1.00	1.00	4.00

Table 9.21: Mean, Median, Minimum and Maximum number of Part-time Professionals (MLS/MLIS) on library's ILL/DD/EDD staff

	Mean	Median	Minimum	Maximum
Entire Sample	0.34	0.00	0.00	1.00

Table 9.22: Mean, Median, Minimum and Maximum number of Part-time Professionals (MLS/MLIS) on library's ILL/DD/EDD staff, Broken Out by Public or Private College

Public or Private	Mean	Median	Minimum	Maximum
Public	0.30	0.00	0.00	1.00
Private	0.46	0.10	0.00	1.00

Table 9.23:   Mean, Median, Minimum and Maximum number of Part-time Professionals (MLS/MLIS) on library's ILL/DD/EDD staff, Broken Out by Type of College

Type of College	Mean	Median	Minimum	Maximum
Community College	0.36	0.00	0.00	1.00
4-Year or M.A. Level	0.30	0.00	0.00	1.00
Ph.D. Level	0.36	0.00	0.00	1.00
Research University	0.33	0.00	0.00	1.00

Table 9.24:   Mean, Median, Minimum and Maximum number of Part-time Professionals (MLS/MLIS) on library's ILL/DD/EDD staff, Broken Out by Country

Country	Mean	Median	Minimum	Maximum
U.S.A.	0.34	0.00	0.00	1.00
Canada	0.38	0.25	0.00	1.00

Table 9.25:   Mean, Median, Minimum and Maximum number of Part-time Professionals (MLS/MLIS) on library's ILL/DD/EDD staff, Broken Out by FTE Enrollment

FTE Enrollment	Mean	Median	Minimum	Maximum
Under 2,000	0.23	0.00	0.00	1.00
2,000-5,000	0.30	0.00	0.00	1.00
5,000+-15,000	0.57	1.00	0.00	1.00
Over 15,000	0.30	0.00	0.00	1.00

Table 9.26:   Mean, Median, Minimum and Maximum number of Part-time Non-Professionals on library's ILL/DD/EDD staff

	Mean	Median	Minimum	Maximum
Entire Sample	0.72	0.75	0.00	4.00

Table 9.27:   Mean, Median, Minimum and Maximum number of Part-time Non-Professionals on library's ILL/DD/EDD staff, Broken Out by Public or Private College

Public or Private	Mean	Median	Minimum	Maximum
Public	0.82	0.75	0.00	4.00
Private	0.60	1.00	0.00	1.00

Table 9.28:   Mean, Median, Minimum and Maximum number of Part-time Non-Professionals on library's ILL/DD/EDD staff, Broken Out by Type of College

Type of College	Mean	Median	Minimum	Maximum
Community College	0.40	0.00	0.00	1.00
4-Year or M.A. Level	0.65	1.00	0.00	1.00
Ph.D. Level	0.81	1.00	0.00	2.25
Research University	1.29	0.63	0.00	4.00

Table 9.29:   Mean, Median, Minimum and Maximum number of Part-time Non-Professionals on library's ILL/DD/EDD staff, Broken Out by Country

Country	Mean	Median	Minimum	Maximum
U.S.A.	0.83	1.00	0.00	4.00
Canada	0.21	0.05	0.00	0.75

Table 9.30:   Mean, Median, Minimum and Maximum number of Part-time Non-Professionals on library's ILL/DD/EDD staff, Broken Out by FTE Enrollment

FTE Enrollment	Mean	Median	Minimum	Maximum
Under 2,000	0.40	0.00	0.00	1.00
2,000-5,000	1.00	1.00	0.00	3.00
5,000+-15,000	0.68	1.00	0.00	1.00
Over 15,000	1.00	0.75	0.00	4.00

Table 9.31:   Mean, Median, Minimum and Maximum number of Student Workers* on library's ILL/DD/EDD staff

	Mean	Median	Minimum	Maximum
Entire Sample	2.07	1.00	0.00	12.00

*(1 position = 10 hours per week)

Table 9.32:   Mean, Median, Minimum and Maximum number of Student Workers* on library's ILL/DD/EDD staff, Broken Out by Public or Private College

Public or Private	Mean	Median	Minimum	Maximum
Public	1.76	1.00	0.00	12.00
Private	2.65	2.00	0.00	10.00

Table 9.33:   Mean, Median, Minimum and Maximum number of Student Workers* on library's ILL/DD/EDD staff, Broken Out by Type of College

Type of College	Mean	Median	Minimum	Maximum
Community College	0.63	0.13	0.00	3.00
4-Year or M.A. Level	2.25	2.00	1.00	5.00
Ph.D. Level	1.84	1.50	0.00	6.00
Research University	3.75	2.50	0.00	12.00

Table 9.34:   Mean, Median, Minimum and Maximum number of Student Workers* on library's ILL/DD/EDD staff, Broken Out by Country

Country	Mean	Median	Minimum	Maximum
U.S.A.	2.12	1.00	0.00	12.00
Canada	1.25	1.00	0.00	3.00

Table 9.35:   Mean, Median, Minimum and Maximum number of Student Workers* on library's ILL/DD/EDD staff, Broken Out by FTE Enrollment

FTE Enrollment	Mean	Median	Minimum	Maximum
Under 2,000	1.58	1.50	0.00	3.00
2,000-5,000	1.48	1.50	0.00	3.50
5,000+-15,000	2.53	2.00	0.00	10.00
Over 15,000	2.45	0.25	0.00	12.00

Table 9.36:   Mean, Median, Minimum and Maximum number of Others on library's ILL/DD/EDD staff

	Mean	Median	Minimum	Maximum
Entire Sample	0.92	0.00	0.00	4.00

Table 9.37:   Mean, Median, Minimum and Maximum number of Others on library's ILL/DD/EDD staff, Broken Out by Public or Private College

Public or Private	Mean	Median	Minimum	Maximum
Public	0.56	0.00	0.00	3.00
Private	1.75	1.50	0.00	4.00

Table 9.38:   Mean, Median, Minimum and Maximum number of Others on library's ILL/DD/EDD staff, Broken Out by Type of College

Type of College	Mean	Median	Minimum	Maximum
Community College	0.33	0.00	0.00	1.00
4-Year or M.A. Level	0.00	0.00	0.00	0.00
Ph.D. Level	2.33	2.00	1.00	4.00
Research University	1.00	0.00	0.00	3.00

Table 9.39: Mean, Median, Minimum and Maximum number of Others on library's ILL/DD/EDD staff, Broken Out by Country

Country	Mean	Median	Minimum	Maximum
U.S.A.	1.09	1.00	0.00	4.00
Canada	0.00	0.00	0.00	0.00

Table 9.40: Mean, Median, Minimum and Maximum number of Others on library's ILL/DD/EDD staff, Broken Out by FTE Enrollment

FTE Enrollment	Mean	Median	Minimum	Maximum
Under 2,000	0.00	0.00	0.00	0.00
2,000-5,000	2.00	1.00	1.00	4.00
5,000+-15,000	1.67	2.00	0.00	3.00
Over 15,000	0.33	0.00	0.00	1.00

What criteria does your institution use to measure staff productivity? For example, turnaround time, number of requests filled per day, etc.? Please list all that are used.

1. Turnaround time and supply statistics from our consortia.

2. No set system in place. Last increase in staff was the result of the end-user survey regarding overall library services.

3. Success in finding requested items; turnaround time; customer satisfaction.

4. Productivity is measured by volume of raw requests received vs. number filled or cancelled.

5. We have not measured productivity beyond maintaining stats, which are compared on a year-by-year basis only.

6. Turnaround time, requests filled.

7. Turnaround time, customer satisfaction, number of requests, adaptability to new technologies.

8. Turnaround time, requests filled, materials shipped.

9. Statistical information and feedback from partner libraries.

10. Both turnaround time and number of raw requests received per day vs. number processed.

11. We check and address ILL items daily with a two-day turnaround time.

12. Not yet done.

13. Requests are filled by need on a daily basis.

14. Turnaround time, number of requests filled per day.

15. Monthly statistics.

16. Turnaround time has been considered toward productivity; increases in borrowing and lending.

17. We have no criteria.

18. Turnaround time.

19. We do look at it; we have looked at internal turnaround time.

20. No productivity studies exist.

21. N/A; too few requests to collect significant data.

22. N/A

23. None.

24. Turnaround time and number of requests filled per day.

25. Turnaround time, processing by username, filled requests.

26. Turnaround time; quality - check number of resend/missed pages, etc.

27. Evaluation process every 6 months looking at all aspects of ILL and direction of library and institutional goals.

28. Number of requests received. I also look at turnaround time to get an idea about efficiency.

29. Annual reports containing overall statistics number of filled and unfilled requests (loans, copies) for lending and borrowing.

30. None.

31. Number of requests submitted and filled.

32. Number of requests processed.

33. We don't measure.

34. Turnaround time.

35. Number of requests filled and unfilled. Turnaround time.

36. Nothing official is maintained. Productivity is based upon how quickly requests are being lent and being processed.

37. Turnaround time would be the criteria that we use.

38. We just get the work done in a timely manner.

39. None, we don't measure it.

40. Turnaround time, number of requests per day/year, fill rate, happy customers.

41. Sweat and the number of prescribed anti-depressants taken.

42. Total volume filled; turnaround time.

43. Turnaround time, volume processed.

44. Turnaround time, fill rate.

45. Turnaround time, number of requests.

46. N/A

47. None.

48. We keep statistics for all the ILL activities. A report is generated once a year.

49. Number of requests lent and borrowed over a month's time. Turnaround time only matters if there are any complaints. Our policy is that any requests from our patrons received before 3pm will go out that same day. Any request from another library will be filled ASAP.

50. None.

51. 1.Turnaround time. 2. Has everything been completed in allocated time.

52. Copyright compliance, efficiency, turnaround time, record-keeping of figures.

53. No measure is used.

54. Patron satisfaction.

55. Turnaround time completing all requests daily.

56. None.

57. N/A

58. Minimally; turnaround time.

Chapter 10: Budgets & Fees

Does your library charge fees for any portion of Interlibrary Loan, Document Delivery, or Electronic Document Delivery? Please explain what fees are charged, and why.

1. No.

2. No.

3. For our users, no charge.

4. Currently we have a two-year pilot project in place where standard ILL fees are covered by the ILL. The end-user is only contacted when the request will incur exceptionally fees.

5. No.

6. No.

7. We provide free ILL service to consortial partners, LVIS libraries and those we have reciprocal agreements with. Fees are charged all others as follows: IFM payment
Loan $5.00   Copy $10.00   Invoiced payment Loan $7.50   Copy $15.00 Higher invoice fees reflect added work required to create invoices and track and handle payments.

8. No.

9. No.

10. No charge for lending of materials.   No charges for borrowing for faculty, staff or students. Community borrowers are charged cost recovery fees for books and journal articles.

11. No.

12. Yes we charge borrowing libraries that do not fall into one of these categories: LVIS, consortial library, reciprocal libraries and those we have historically provided free service to such as local colleges, local governmental and state agencies. Loan fees are currently $7.50 if invoiced $5 if IFM. Copy fees are currently $15 if invoiced and $10 if IFM. A higher fee is charged for generating an invoice, processing checks, management of invoices, etc.

13. Yes, occasionally.

14. Charge $10 to non-state borrowers, we do not pass on costs to our students, faculty or staff.

15. Yes, we charge our patrons $1 for borrowed articles and $1 a day for overdue ILL books. We do not charge other libraries to borrow/lend.

16. No.

17. No.

18. Fees to community patrons for returning books.

19. IFM/Invoice for out-of-state Transactions.

20. No charge for loans or photocopies.

21. We will charge general public for a photocopy ILL.

22. 25$ and less - covered by library; if more, the user pays.

23. We do not charge our patrons but we do charge fees to other libraries for materials we supply. Fees are based on consortial agreements.

24. No. We only charge the patron who wants to buy a dissertation (the cost of the dissertation) via Dissertation Express and use our services as intermediary.

25. We have very few requests for our collection so we charge minimal fees 0-$5. Most of our ILLs are to other libraries.

26. No.

27. No.

28. No.

29. We only charge if a patron wants to purchase a photocopy of a dissertation.

30. We do not charge.

31. For borrowing, only the Friends of the Library users are responsible for borrowing fees. For lending, we reciprocate and only charge those libraries that charge us. It was decided two years ago not to charge libraries in state, as we are a state institution.

32. To offset cost of delivery and processing, fees are charged to out-of-province libraries for both photocopies and books. In province, a fee is charged only for photocopies.

33. No fees.

34. Yes. $1.00 for materials requested by our patrons. We are an LVIS participant. As a rule we do not charge.

35. Only charge a fee if there are no free sources and the patron agrees to pay.

36. No.

37. No.

38. No fees.

39. No.

40. If a library charges us to borrow an item, we pass that charge on to the patron.

41. Yes, Library is a reciprocal Lender and charges for supplying materials to non-lenders and special handling, i.e.: RUSH or overnight Delivery.

42. We charge libraries that charge us. Our patrons are charged a fee only if there is a cost involved.

43. We do not charge our patrons. We charge libraries outside of GA to borrow Special Collections Microfilm and charge libraries outside of our groups. This helps account for some of the costs we incur with loaning items.

44. Fees are charged to non-Freeshare requestors.

45. Yes. Whenever we are charged, we charge the patron.

46. No.

47. Generally no fees are charged for most university departments. One department that belongs to our main campus has all costs charged back to the main campus library. We charge our affiliations, USGS, NOAA, etc., a set fee that is determined by negotiation every few years.

48. No.

49. None whatsoever.

50. No.

51. We charge $10.00 per transaction for only those libraries that charge us for ILLs.

52. No.

53. Yes, charge for dissertations ordered.

54. No.

55. No.

56. No.

57. No.

58. No, it is a service for our students.

59. No.

60. No.

61. No.

62. No.

63. No fees.

64. No charges at any time.

65. No.

66. No.

67. Usually not. Occasionally a fee is requested if the charge exceeds our IFM or unusual material requested by undergraduates. $.10/page for copies, $1.00 for loans. Faculty not charged No extra charge for Distance Education patrons.

68. Fees are only charged if lender charges - then those charges are passed on to the borrower. We do not charge to borrow or lend items except for photocopies from "The Morgue," our index to mortuary science journals, which is used by most mortuary schools in the U.S.

69. We offer our borrowers the opportunity to pay any charges incurred by a loaning library before accepting the loan.

70. Only if sending by First Class Airmail overseas, or if overnight shipping or two-day shipping is required.

71. No.

Table 10.1:   Mean, Median, Minimum and Maximum current annual budget for library's ILL/DD/EDD operations*

	Mean	Median	Minimum	Maximum
Entire Sample	14,107.06	6,000.00	0.00	105,578.00

*excluding staff costs but including automation costs, copyright costs, material costs and other operating costs

Table 10.2:   Mean, Median, Minimum and Maximum current annual budget for library's ILL/DD/EDD operations*, Broken Out by Public or Private College

Public or Private	Mean	Median	Minimum	Maximum
Public	18,770.59	7,098.00	100.00	105,578.00
Private	6,732.83	5,000.00	780.00	17,000.00

Table 10.3:   Mean, Median, Minimum and Maximum current annual budget for library's ILL/DD/EDD operations*, Broken Out by Type of College

Type of College	Mean	Median	Minimum	Maximum
Community College	3,004.00	3,000.00	100.00	10,000.00
4-Year or M.A. Level	7,229.40	6,500.00	780.00	17,000.00
Ph.D. Level	24,642.86	12,000.00	5,000.00	85,000.00
Research University	27,739.63	9,000.00	600.00	105,578.00

Table 10.4: Mean, Median, Minimum and Maximum current annual budget for library's ILL/DD/EDD operations*, Broken Out by Country

Country	Mean	Median	Minimum	Maximum
U.S.A.	14,325.88	8,500.00	100.00	85,000.00
Canada	16,325.00	3,513.00	200.00	105,578.00

Table 10.5: Mean, Median, Minimum and Maximum current annual budget for library's ILL/DD/EDD operations*, Broken Out by FTE Enrollment

FTE Enrollment	Mean	Median	Minimum	Maximum
Under 2,000	3,508.89	3,000.00	600.00	10,000.00
2,000-5,000	6,430.00	5,000.00	100.00	17,000.00
5,000+-15,000	15,000.00	9,750.00	5,000.00	40,000.00
Over 15,000	33,394.63	6,857.50	125.00	105,578.00

Table 10.6: Mean, Median, Minimum and Maximum percentage change in library's ILL/DD/EDD budget over the past year

	Mean	Median	Minimum	Maximum
Entire Sample	2.40	0.00	-20.00	50.00

Table 10.7: Mean, Median, Minimum and Maximum percentage change in library's ILL/DD/EDD budget over the past year, Broken Out by Public or Private College

Public or Private	Mean	Median	Minimum	Maximum
Public	2.86	0.00	-20.00	50.00
Private	2.18	0.00	-1.00	25.00

Table 10.8: Mean, Median, Minimum and Maximum percentage change in library's ILL/DD/EDD budget over the past year, Broken Out by Type of College

Type of College	Mean	Median	Minimum	Maximum
Community College	-2.10	0.00	-20.00	0.00
4-Year or M.A. Level	3.78	0.00	-1.00	25.00
Ph.D. Level	4.88	0.00	0.00	24.00
Research University	6.40	0.00	-13.00	50.00

Table 10.9: Mean, Median, Minimum and Maximum percentage change in library's ILL/DD/EDD budget over the past year, Broken Out by Country

Country	Mean	Median	Minimum	Maximum
U.S.A.	3.63	0.00	-20.00	50.00
Canada	-0.43	0.00	-13.00	10.00

Table 10.10: Mean, Median, Minimum and Maximum percentage change in library's ILL/DD/EDD budget over the past year, Broken Out by FTE Enrollment

FTE Enrollment	Mean	Median	Minimum	Maximum
Under 2,000	0.44	0.00	-20.00	25.00
2,000-5,000	1.29	0.00	-1.00	10.00
5,000+-15,000	3.78	0.00	-5.00	24.00
Over 15,000	5.29	0.00	-13.00	50.00

Table 10.11: Mean, Median, Minimum and Maximum percentage change expected in library's ILL/DD/EDD budget over the next year

	Mean	Median	Minimum	Maximum
Entire Sample	5.41	0.00	-20.00	75.00

Table 10.12: Mean, Median, Minimum and Maximum percentage change expected in library's ILL/DD/EDD budget over the next year, Broken Out by Public or Private College

Public or Private	Mean	Median	Minimum	Maximum
Public	4.09	0.00	-20.00	50.00
Private	9.17	0.00	0.00	75.00

Table 10.13: Mean, Median, Minimum and Maximum percentage change expected in library's ILL/DD/EDD budget over the next year, Broken Out by Type of College

Type of College	Mean	Median	Minimum	Maximum
Community College	1.11	0.00	0.00	10.00
4-Year or M.A. Level	6.82	0.00	0.00	50.00
Ph.D. Level	12.22	5.00	-20.00	75.00
Research University	1.00	0.00	-5.00	10.00

Table 10.14: Mean, Median, Minimum and Maximum percentage change expected in library's ILL/DD/EDD budget over the next year, Broken Out by Country

Country	Mean	Median	Minimum	Maximum
U.S.A.	3.27	0.00	-20.00	50.00
Canada	5.71	0.00	0.00	20.00

Table 10.15: Mean, Median, Minimum and Maximum percentage change expected in library's budget over the next year, Broken Out by FTE Enrollment

FTE Enrollment	Mean	Median	Minimum	Maximum
Under 2,000	3.89	0.00	0.00	25.00
2,000-5,000	2.86	0.00	0.00	20.00
5,000+-15,000	13.00	0.00	-20.00	75.00
Over 15,000	1.88	0.00	0.00	10.00

Table 10.16: Mean, Median, Minimum and Maximum total annual fee revenues for ILL/EDD/DD in the past year

	Mean	Median	Minimum	Maximum
Entire Sample	1,443.57	0.00	0.00	8,300.00

Table 10.17: Mean, Median, Minimum and Maximum total annual fee revenues for ILL/EDD/DD in the past year, Broken Out by Public or Private College

Public or Private	Mean	Median	Minimum	Maximum
Public	1,728.89	66.00	0.00	8,300.00
Private	930.00	0.00	0.00	5000.00

Table 10.18: Mean, Median, Minimum and Maximum total annual fee revenues for ILL/EDD/DD in the past year, Broken Out by Type of College

Type of College	Mean	Median	Minimum	Maximum
Community College	14.67	0.00	0.00	82.00
4-Year or M.A. Level	0.00	0.00	0.00	0.00
Ph.D. Level	2,825.80	1,700.00	0.00	8,300.00
Research University	3,007.50	3,000.00	0.00	6030.00

Table 10.19: Mean, Median, Minimum and Maximum total annual fee revenues for ILL/EDD/DD in the past year, Broken Out by Country

Country	Mean	Median	Minimum	Maximum
U.S.A.	1,374.26	0.00	0.00	8,300.00
Canada	1,762.40	82.00	0.00	6,030.00

Table 10.20: Mean, Median, Minimum and Maximum total annual fee revenues for ILL/EDD/DD in the past year, Broken Out by FTE Enrollment

FTE Enrollment	Mean	Median	Minimum	Maximum
Under 2,000	0.00	0.00	0.00	0.00
2,000-5,000	792.44	0.00	0.00	4,300.00
5,000+-15,000	3,794.00	4,000.00	0.00	8,300.00
Over 15,000	1,121.67	0.00	0.00	6,030.00

Table 10.21:   Percentage of library managements that expect ILL/DD/EDD services to

	We don't really charge for document delivery or ILL	Defray some of the costs but definitely less than half	Defray more than half the costs exclusive of salaries and overhead	More or less pay for itself exclusive of salaries and overhead	Pretty much completely pay for itself including salaries and overhead	Pay completely for itself and produce a surplus for the library for use in other areas
Entire Sample	72.60%	19.18%	1.37%	2.74%	0.00%	4.11%

Table 10.22:   Percentage of library managements that expect ILL/DD/EDD services to, Broken Out by Public or Private College

Public or Private	We don't really charge for document delivery or ILL	Defray some of the costs but definitely less than half	Defray more than half the costs exclusive of salaries and overhead	More or less pay for itself exclusive of salaries and overhead	Pretty much completely pay for itself including salaries and overhead	Pay completely for itself and produce a surplus for the library for use in other areas
Public	73.47%	16.33%	2.04%	4.08%	0.00%	4.08%
Private	70.83%	25.00%	0.00%	0.00%	0.00%	4.17%

Table 10.23:   Percentage of library managements that expect ILL/DD/EDD services to, Broken Out by Type of College

Type of College	We don't really charge for document delivery or ILL	Defray some of the costs but definitely less than half	Defray more than half the costs exclusive of salaries and overhead	More or less pay for itself exclusive of salaries and overhead	Pretty much completely pay for itself including salaries and overhead	Pay completely for itself and produce a surplus for the library for use in other areas
Community College	90.91%	4.55%	0.00%	0.00%	0.00%	4.55%
4-Year or M.A. Level	92.31%	7.69%	0.00%	0.00%	0.00%	0.00%
Ph.D. Level	43.48%	43.48%	4.35%	4.35%	0.00%	4.35%
Research University	73.33%	13.33%	0.00%	6.67%	0.00%	6.67%

Table 10.24: Percentage of library managements that expect ILL/DD/EDD services to, Broken Out by Country

Country	We don't really charge for document delivery or ILL	Defray some of the costs but definitely less than half	Defray more than half the costs exclusive of salaries and overhead	More or less pay for itself exclusive of salaries and overhead	Pretty much completely pay for itself including salaries and overhead	Pay completely for itself and produce a surplus for the library for use in other areas
U.S.A.	73.77%	18.03%	0.00%	3.28%	0.00%	4.92%
Canada	72.73%	18.18%	9.09%	0.00%	0.00%	0.00%

Table 10.25: Percentage of library managements that expect ILL/DD/EDD services to, Broken Out by FTE Enrollment

FTE Enrollment	We don't really charge for document delivery or ILL	Defray some of the costs but definitely less than half	Defray more than half the costs exclusive of salaries and overhead	More or less pay for itself exclusive of salaries and overhead	Pretty much completely pay for itself including salaries and overhead	Pay completely for itself and produce a surplus for the library for use in other areas
Under 2,000	100.00%	0.00%	0.00%	0.00%	0.00%	0.00%
2,000-5,000	68.42%	26.32%	5.26%	0.00%	0.00%	0.00%
5,000+-15,000	66.67%	20.83%	0.00%	0.00%	0.00%	12.50%
Over 15,000	64.71%	23.53%	0.00%	11.76%	0.00%	0.00%

Table 10.26: Percentage of libraries whose ILL/DD/EDD operation works from "unit costs" in order to determine budget needs and work productivity

	Yes	No
Entire Sample	4.23%	95.77%

Table 10.27: Percentage of libraries whose ILL/DD/EDD operation works from "unit costs" in order to determine budget needs and work productivity, Broken Out by Public or Private College

Public or Private	Yes	No
Public	4.26%	95.74%
Private	4.17%	95.83%

184

Table 10.28: **Percentage of libraries whose ILL/DD/EDD operation works from "unit costs" in order to determine budget needs and work productivity, Broken Out by Type of College**

Type of College	Yes	No
Community College	0.00%	100.00%
4-Year or M.A. Level	0.00%	100.00%
Ph.D. Level	4.35%	95.65%
Research University	15.38%	84.62%

Table 10.29: **Percentage of libraries whose ILL/DD/EDD operation works from "unit costs" in order to determine budget needs and work productivity, Broken Out by Country**

Country	Yes	No
U.S.A.	3.33%	96.67%
Canada	10.00%	90.00%

Table 10.30: **Percentage of libraries whose ILL/DD/EDD operation works from "unit costs" in order to determine budget needs and work productivity, Broken Out by FTE Enrollment**

FTE Enrollment	Yes	No
Under 2,000	0.00%	100.00%
2,000-5,000	5.56%	94.44%
5,000+-15,000	8.33%	91.67%
Over 15,000	0.00%	100.00%

Chapter 11: Distance Learning and ILL

Table 11.1: Mean, Median, Minimum and Maximum percentage of library's interlibrary loan request volume (from other institutions to your library) that is accounted for by requests from college's distance learning students or instructors

	Mean	Median	Minimum	Maximum
Entire Sample	8.25	2.00	-5.00	100.00

Table 11.2: Mean, Median, Minimum and Maximum percentage of library's interlibrary loan request volume (from other institutions to your library) that is accounted for by requests from college's distance learning students or instructors, Broken Out by Public or Private College

Public or Private	Mean	Median	Minimum	Maximum
Public	8.45	3.25	-5.00	100.00
Private	7.92	2.00	0.00	25.00

Table 11.3: Mean, Median, Minimum and Maximum percentage of library's interlibrary loan request volume (from other institutions to your library) that is accounted for by requests from college's distance learning students or instructors, Broken Out by Type of College

Type of College	Mean	Median	Minimum	Maximum
Community College	4.45	3.25	-5.00	15.00
4-Year or M.A. Level	1.00	1.00	0.00	2.00
Ph.D. Level	15.76	6.25	0.00	100.00
Research University	8.08	6.25	0.00	25.00

Table 11.4: Mean, Median, Minimum and Maximum percentage of library's interlibrary loan request volume (from other institutions to your library) that is accounted for by requests from college's distance learning students or instructors, Broken Out by Country

Country	Mean	Median	Minimum	Maximum
U.S.A.	5.58	1.50	-5.00	29.00
Canada	21.26	10.00	0.80	100.00

Table 11.5:   Mean, Median, Minimum and Maximum percentage of library's interlibrary loan request volume (from other institutions to your library) that is accounted for by requests from college's distance learning students or instructors, Broken Out by FTE Enrollment

FTE Enrollment	Mean	Median	Minimum	Maximum
Under 2,000	2.13	0.00	-5.00	15.00
2,000-5,000	6.51	2.00	0.80	25.00
5,000+-15,000	9.92	7.50	0.00	29.00
Over 15,000	13.42	2.50	0.00	100.00

Please comment on how, or if, your institution's distance learning programs have affected your ILL/DD/EDD operations and statistics.

1. Increase in students creates commensurate increase in ILL services.

2. N/A

3. N/A

4. Increase in journal article requests.

5. When we took over service to distance learners several years ago, we saw a spike in use. Over the years and with refinement of professional support for distance users and a dramatic increase in electronic resources available to them, the demand for ILL and DD has fallen.

6. No significant impact yet; however, we anticipate distance learning students will account for higher percentage of ILL service in future with the biggest implication being shipping cost, which we currently absorb.

7. Not so much.

8. Very little impact.

9. Minimal impact.

10. It is still a new program. Much of the material they seek is available though our electronic journal center.

11. There is a policy regarding distance learning, although it is rarely used due to time.

12. The distance learning programs have increased ILL operations and statistics. Students, faculty and staff tend to use ILL to request materials owned by the library. This has caused more work and has skewed some of the statistics for ILL and DD.

13. No extra effect.

14. N/A

15. There has been little effect.

16. Difficult at this point because policies not fully established. Attempting to do more online reserves for universal timely access but licenses and copyright laws interfere.

17. We give DE students the same privileges as on-campus students for ILL/Doc Del.

18. Very little. DD students are more likely to request items that we need to purchase, rather than borrow, such as case studies and working papers, or even books to some extent.

19. Our distance learning program is large but it has not affected our ILLs.

20. N/A

21. Not very much.

22. Most distance students are not enrolled in research-intensive coursework and request little on Interlibrary Loan.

23. They are normally affected on the ILL statistics as requests from others?

24. Unfortunately, there is no cooperative service.

25. N/A

26. It indicated a stronger need for electronic delivery and probably increases our statistics slightly.

27. N/A

28. None.

29. Very little.

30. Very little.

31. Distance learning has affected the ILL operations and statistics very little.

32. N/A

33. Distance Learning programs have not significantly affected our ILL operations or statistics.

34. Distance learning students don't use interlibrary loan here very much.

35. None yet.

36. No effect.

37. It has not affected out ILL/DD operations or statistics. The DE students make up an extremely small percentage of our ILL population. It is a fairly new venture here for our faculty and the institution. I think they (the faculty) generally provide the majority of materials needed to their students. Those that do need materials seek us, but generally are in need of articles which are filtered through and delivered electronically through their ILLiad account. No big impact. We treat them like our document delivery customers, with the exception of book pick-up here at Nazareth.

38. Not much of an effect.

39. Definitely grown over past three years.

40. At this time not very much at all.

41. N/A

42. N/A

43. No measurable effect.

44. Not significantly.

45. Has not affected.

46. No distance learning program.

47. Has not affected it.

48. No major effect.

49. We have seen only minimal increase.

50. N/A

Free access to research and data on the Internet has dramatically increased, examples of which include the WorldWideScience.org portal that was launched in 2007, federal Open Access initiatives, Google books, and other mass digitization projects. Scholarly communications are increasingly moving online, and leaving, to some degree, the print environment. Please explain how, or if, this has affected your DD, EDD and ILL workflows and activities.

1. Noticeable increase in fulltext article ILLs.

2. ILL seems to be static at the moment in terms of volume. My guess is that although a great deal more information is available as described above without going through ILL, this is offset by users' ability to discover the existence of much more information for which they still do need ILL.

3. Although Internet access has allowed users to obtain material without our service, it has also increased our numbers as end-users are aware that items exist.

4. Some online resources are not available for interlibrary loan, which causes us to spend more time to find items.

5. We find that when citations are incomplete or appear to be wrong, Google is a good, quick and easy way to confirm data without needing to try and guess which databases the patron was using. We also find a growing number of requested items natively published or otherwise openly available on the Internet. We direct our users to these whenever possible.

6. ILL has steadily decreased in volume with the rise of digital content and will likely continue in future. One change to our activities is an increase in instruction to our patrons on how to access digital content in our databases. Increasingly patrons submit ILL requests for material that we own but is not easily found through traditional tools like our catalog.

7. People still have lots of items they cannot obtain themselves even with the Internet craze.

8. This hasn't really affected workflows and activities.

9. Probable increase, but we don't keep statistics.

10. Uncertain.

11. Frequently, staff are checking for unfilled ILL requests on search engines and other sources to ascertain whether access is possible via open access resources.

12. It has not affected our ILLs largely due to the information literacy of our patrons.

13. This has increased our access to information for our students but caused more work for us as we look for fulltext.

14. Increased the borrowers' awareness of materials they would like to have; they don't always check for online articles that are available.

15. Probably balances out; I find more on the web for ILLs, but I also get more requests from students because this research and data is freely available on the web. For example, a student or faculty member will become aware of an ebook, but ask for the paper edition through ILL.

16. We have yet to feel the effects of this.

17. Hasn't affected us much as faculty and infolit trainers emphasize difficulties with web materials, e.g., explain peer review process.

18. It has facilitated the delivery of non-returnables but has not affected the delivery of returnables.

19. There has been a slight decrease in borrowing requests, but we cannot determine if the reason for that is the profusion of information available online or whether there are other reasons.

20. For the past three years the number of requests has remained steady, so I would have to say that it has not affected our ILLs.

21. N/A

22. I haven't seen a change.

23. Some of the students are more familiar with this than some of the teachers.

24. I think the increase in items available online has greatly reduced our borrowing statistics.

25. Yes, especially for articles request. We found many fulltext available online to the public and guide our patron to the articles without having to borrow from the lending libraries.

26. It has increased the service, and resources are being identified or found on the Internet that often charge. Our ILL services are then used to obtain.

27. Has decreased the volume of requests. Increase in the amount of time spent locating materials available on the net.

28. It does not appear to affect our usage. Our statistics are significantly up for the last two years.

29. Unknown. However, I would assume that it might decrease the numbers a bit.

30. Definitely has affected ILL workflow. All requests are screened for online availability before submitting the request to OCLC.

31. Not really, we are not a big ILL, DD, EDD institution.

32. Requests for this type of material are down.

33. On occasion, I check some of these sources before requesting an item.

34. Primary users are graduate students and faculty. Materials requested tend to be more research-based and not available via electronic resources. The web has assisted those individuals to identify materials but find they are fee-based or unavailable. Being able to find references to materials, but not the resources themselves, continues to drive increased demand for ILL services.

35. These services have decreased slightly. There has been no real impact.

36. Not enough at this point for the types of items that our patrons are looking for.

37. No effect.

38. This hasn't affected us that much. People seem to want the printed book. I think what has hurt us is that professors don't require books as much anymore for basic research. Therefore, our volume of interlibrary loan for books has gone down.

39. N/A

40. We used to be a net borrower. We have moved to being a net lender. We once lent mostly to our other campuses. We now lend mostly to libraries outside our university.

41. Requests for articles from journals about half of what it was five years ago.

42. This has greatly improved our ability to 'fill' those harder-to-locate or acquire materials (such as rare manuscripts now available online). This is a wonderful advancement and we hope to see more. It has not affected our workflow, as we send the customer the link into the item, or deliver it electronically if applicable/allowable.

43. Decreased relative need.

44. ILL has increased.

45. Improved turnaround time.

46. It has not affected ILL workflows.

47. Remained the same.

48. N/A

49. We noticed a large jump in ILL book lending requests when our catalog was included in OCLC Worldcat.

50. This has not really affected the ILL workflow.

51. Our patrons do have more access to fulltext articles. However, they also have more access to online databases that we do not have a subscription to. So, in a way, technological advancements have balanced each other out.

52. Has had a positive effect on workflow and load.

53. Not sure how it may have affected ILL as our numbers remain the same or have increased.

54. Not a significant impact...information on the Internet is scholastically correct or verifiable in many cases.

55. No effect noted.

56. We receive more requests.

57. Very little effect.

58. Looks like this year our volume will be down by about 50%.

59. Have not seen any increase.

60. We rarely have to request an article from a periodical anymore. We have access to approx. 100 databases.

61. We do check the Internet regularly for online availability of fulltext articles, after we've checked our local holdings and eholdings. This has reduced ILL requests but bumped up DD and EDD considerably.

OTHER REPORTS FROM PRIMARY RESEARCH GROUP INC.

THE INTERNATIONAL SURVEY OF LIBRARY & MUSEUM DIGITIZATION PROJECTS
ISBN: 1-57440-105-X   **Price: $89.50**   **October 2008**

The International Survey of Library & Museum Digitization Projects presents detailed data about the management and development of a broad range of library special collection and museum digitization projects. Data are broken out by type of digitization project (i.e., text, photograph, film, audio, etc.) size and type of institution, annual spending on digitization and other variables. The report presents data and narrative on staffing, training, funding, technology selection, outsourcing, permissions and copyright clearance, cataloging, digital asset management, software and applications selection, marketing and many other issues of interest to libraries and museums that are digitizing aspects of their collections.

THE SURVEY OF ACADEMIC & RESEARCH LIBRARY JOURNAL PURCHASING PRACTICES
ISBN: 1-57440-108-4   **Price: $89.50**   **November 2008**

This report looks closely at the acquisition practices for scientific, technical and academic journals of academic and research libraries. Some of the many issues covered: attitudes toward the pricing and digital access policies of select major journals publishers, preferences for print, print/electronic access combinations, and electronic access alone arrangements. Covers spending plans, preferences for use of consortiums, and use of, and evaluation of subscription agents. Charts attitudes toward CLOCKSS, open access, use of URL resolvers and other pressing issues of interest to major purchasers of academic and technical journals.

ACADEMIC LIBRARY CATALOGING PRACTICES BENCHMARKS
ISBN: 1-57440-106-8   **Price: $89.50**   **November 2008**

This 254-page report presents data from a survey of the cataloging practices of approximately 80 North American academic libraries. In more than 630 tables of data and related commentary from participating librarians and our analysts, the report gives a broad overview of academic library cataloging practices related to outsourcing, selection and deployment of personnel, salaries, the state of continuing education in cataloging, and much more. Data are broken out by size and type of college and for public and private colleges. Survey participants also discuss how they define the cataloger's range of responsibilities, how they train their catalogers, how they assess cataloging quality, whether they use cataloging quotas or other measures to spur productivity, what software and other cataloging technology they use and why, how they make outsourcing decisions and more.

SURVEY OF ACADEMIC LIBRARY USE OF INSTRUCTIONAL TECHNOLOGY:
ISBN: 1-57440-107-6   Price: $85.00   October 2008

The Survey of Academic Library Use of Instructional Technology examines use of information literacy computer labs, classroom response "clicker" technology, whiteboards, and many other educational technologies used by libraries. In an era in which library education has become an increasingly important part of the academic librarian's duties, this report provides insights on how peer institutions are allocating their educational budgets and choosing the most effective technologies and practices in information and general library literacy.

CORPORATE LIBRARY BENCHMARKS, 2009 Edition
ISBN 1-57440-109-2   Publication Date: December 2008 Price: $195.00

Corporate Library Benchmarks, 2009 Edition presents extensive data from 52 corporate and other business-oriented libraries; data is broken out by company size, type of industry and other criteria.

The mean number of employees for the organizations in the sample is 16,000; the median, 1700. Some of the many issues covered in the report are: spending on electronic and print forms of books, directories, journals and other information resources; library staffing trends, number of library locations maintained and the allocation of office space to the library, disputes with publishers, allocation of library staff time, level of awareness of database contract terms of peer institutions, reference workload, and the overall level of influence of the library in corporate decision making.

LIBRARY USE OF E-BOOKS
ISBN: 1-57440-101-7 Price: $75.00   Publication Date: April 2008

Data in the report are based on a survey of 75 academic, public and special libraries. Data are broken out by library budget size, for U.S. and non-U.S. libraries and for academic and non-academic libraries. The report presents more than 300 tables of data on e-book use by libraries, as well as analysis and commentary. Librarians detail their plans on how they plan to develop their e-book collections, what they think of e-book readers and software, and which e-book aggregators and publishers appeal to them most and why. Other issues covered include: library production of e-books and collection digitization, e-book collection information literacy efforts, use of e-books in course reserves and inter-library loan, e-book pricing and inflation issues, acquisition sources and strategies for e-books and other issues of concern to libraries and book publishers.

LAW LIBRARY BENCHMARKS, 2008-09 EDITION
ISBN: 1-57440-104-1   Price: $129.00   Publication Date: October 2008

Data in the report are based on a survey of 55 North American law libraries drawn from law firm, private company, university, courthouse and government agency law libraries. Data are broken out by size and type of library for ease in benchmarking. The 120+ page report covers developments in staffing, salaries, budgets, materials spending, use of blogs

& wikis, use of legal directories, the library role in knowledge management, records management and content management systems. Patron and librarian training, reimbursement for library-related education and other issues are also covered in this latest edition.

RESEARCH LIBRARY INTERNATIONAL BENCHMARKS
ISBN: 1-57440-103-3   Publication Date: June 2008   Price: $95.00

Research Library International Benchmarks presents data from a survey of 45 major research libraries from the U.S., Australia, Canada, Spain, the U.K., Japan and others. Data are presented separately for university, government/non-profit and corporate/legal libraries, and for U.S. and non-U.S. libraries, as well as by size of library and type of library, corporate/legal, university and government. The 200-page report presents a broad range of data on current and planned materials, salary, info technology and capital spending, hiring plans, spending trends for e-books, journals, books and much, much more. Provides data on trends in discount margins from vendors, relations with consortiums, information literacy efforts, workstation, laptop and learning space development, use of scanners and digital cameras, use of RFID technology, federated search and many other pressing issues for major research libraries, university and otherwise.

THE SURVEY OF LIBRARY DATABASE LICENSING PRACTICES
ISBN: 1-57440-093-2   Price: $80.00   Publication Date: December 2007

The study presents data from 90 libraries – corporate, legal, college, public, state and nonprofit libraries – about their database licensing practices. More than half of the participating libraries are from the U.S., and the rest are from Canada, Australia, the U.K. and other countries. Data are broken out by library type and size of library, as well as for overall level of database expenditure. The 100+-page study, with more than 400 tables and charts, presents benchmarking data enabling librarians to compare their library's practices to peers in many areas related to licensing. Metrics provided include: percentage of licenses from consortiums, spending on consortium dues, time spent seeking new consortium partners, number of consortium memberships maintained; growth rate in the percentage of licenses obtained through consortiums; expectation for consortium purchases in the future; number of licenses, growth rate in the number of licenses, spending on licenses for directories, electronic journals, e-books and magazine/newspaper databases; future spending plans on all of the above; price inflation experienced for electronic resources in business, medical, humanities, financial, market research, social sciences and many other information categories; price inflation for e-books, electronic directories, journals and newspaper/magazine databases; percentage of licenses that require passwords; percentage of licenses that have simultaneous access restrictions; spending on legal services related to licenses; and much more.

THE INTERNATIONAL SURVEY OF INSTITUTIONAL DIGITAL REPOSITORIES
ISBN: 1-57440-090-8   Price: $89.50   Publication Date: November 2007

The study presents data from 56 institutional digital repositories from 11 countries, including the U.S., Canada, Australia, Germany, South Africa, India, Turkey and other countries. The 121-page study presents more than 300 tables of data and commentary and is based on data from higher education libraries and other institutions involved in institutional digital repository development. In more than 300 tables and associated commentary, the report describes norms and benchmarks for budgets, software use, manpower needs and deployment, financing, usage, marketing and other facets of the management of international digital repositories. The report helps to answer questions such as: who contributes to the repositories and on what terms? Who uses the repositories? What do they contain and how fast are they growing in terms of content and end use? What measures have repositories used to gain faculty and other researcher participation? How successful have these methods been? How has the repository been marketed and cataloged? What has been the financial impact? Data are broken out by size and type of institution for easier benchmarking.

PREVAILING & BEST PRACTICES IN ELECTRONIC AND PRINT SERIALS MANAGEMENT
ISBN: 1-57440-076-2   Price: $80.00   Publication Date: November 2005

This report looks closely at the electronic and print serials procurement and management practices of 11 libraries, including: the University of Ohio, Villanova University, the Colorado School of Mines, Carleton College, Northwestern University, Baylor University, Princeton University, the University of Pennsylvania, the University of San Francisco, Embry-Riddle Aeronautical University and the University of Nebraska Medical Center. The report looks at both electronic and print serials and includes discussions of the following issues: selection and management of serials agents, including the negotiation of payment; allocating the serials budget by department; resolving access issues with publishers; use of consortiums in journal licensing; invoice reconciliation and payment; periodicals binding, claims, check-in and management; serials department staff size and range of responsibilities; serials management software; use of open access archives and university depositories; policies on gift subscriptions, free trials and academic exchanges of publications; use of electronic serials/catalog linking technology; acquisition of usage statistics; cooperative arrangements with other local libraries and other issues in serials management.

CORPORATE LIBRARY BENCHMARKS, 2007 Edition
ISBN: 1-57440-084-3   Price: $189.00

This report, our sixth survey of corporate libraries, presents a broad range of data, broken out by size and type of organization. Among the issues covered are: spending trends on books, magazines, journals, databases, CD-ROMs, directories and other information vehicles, plans to augment or reduce the scope and size of the corporate library, hiring plans, salary spending and personnel use, librarian research priorities by type of subject matter, policies on information literacy and library education, library relations with management, budget trends, breakdown in spending by the library versus other corporate departments that procure information, librarian use of blogs and RSS feeds, level of discounts received from book jobbers, use of subscription agents, and other issues of concern to corporate and other business librarians.

EMERGING ISSUES IN ACADEMIC LIBRARY CATALOGING & TECHNICAL SERVICES
ISBN: 1-57440-086-X   Price: $72.50   Publication Date: April 2007
This report presents nine highly detailed case studies of leading university cataloging and technical service departments. It provides insights into how they are handling 10 major changes facing them, including: the encouragement of cataloging productivity; impact of new technologies on and enhancement of online catalogs; the transition to metadata standards; the cataloging of Websites and digital and other special collections; library catalog and metadata training; database maintenance, holdings and physical processing; managing the relationship with acquisitions departments; staff education; and other important issues. Survey participants represent academic libraries of varying sizes and classifications, with many different viewpoints. Universities surveyed are: Brigham Young; Curry College; Haverford College; Illinois, Louisiana and Pennsylvania State Universities; University of North Dakota; University of Washington; and Yale University.

THE MARKETING OF HISTORIC SITES, MUSEUMS, EXHIBITS AND ARCHIVES
ISBN: 1-57440-074-6   Price: $95.00   Publication Date: June 2005
This report looks closely at how history is presented and marketed by organizations such as history museums, libraries, historical societies, and historic sites and monuments. The report profiles the efforts of the Vermont Historical Society, Hook's Historic Drug Store and Pharmacy, the Thomas Jefferson Foundation/Monticello, the Musee Conti Wax Museum of New Orleans, the Bostonian Society, the Dittrick Medical History Center, the Band Museum, the Belmont Mansion, the Kansas State Historical Society, the Computer History Museum, the Atari Virtual Museum, the Museum of American Financial History, the Atlanta History Center and the public libraries of Denver and Evansville. The study's revealing profiles, based on extensive interviews with executive directors and marketing managers of the institutions cited, provide a deeply detailed look at how history museums, sites, societies and monuments are marketing themselves.

LICENSING AND COPYRIGHT MANAGEMENT: BEST PRACTICES OF COLLEGE, SPECIAL AND RESEARCH LIBRARIES
ISBN: 1-57440-068-1   Price: $80   Publication Date: May 2004
This report looks closely at the licensing and copyright-management strategies of a sample of leading research, college and special libraries and consortiums and includes interviews with leading experts. The focus is on electronic-database licensing, and includes discussions of the most pressing issues: development of consortiums and group buying initiatives, terms of access, liability for infringement, archiving, training and development, free-trial periods, contract language, contract-management software and

time-management issues, acquiring and using usage statistics, elimination of duplication, enhancement of bargaining power, open-access publishing policies, interruption-of-service contingency arrangements, changes in pricing over the life of the contract, interlibrary loan of electronic files, copyright clearance, negotiating tactics, uses of consortiums, and many other issues. The report profiles the emergence of consortiums and group-buying arrangements.

TRENDS IN TRAINING COLLEGE FACULTY, STUDENTS & STAFF IN COMPUTER LITERACY
ISBN: 1-57440-085-1   Price: $67.50   Publication Date: April 2007

This report looks closely at how nine institutions of higher education are approaching the question of training faculty, staff and students in the use of educationally oriented information technologies. The report helps answer questions such as: what is the most productive way to help faculty master new information technologies? How much should be spent on such training? What are the best practices? How should distance learning instructors be trained? How formal, and how ad-hoc, should training efforts be? What should computer literacy standards be among students? How can subject-specific computer literacy be integrated into curriculums? Should colleges develop their own training methods, buy packaged solutions, find them on the Web?

Organizations profiled are: Brooklyn Law School, Florida State University College of Medicine, Indiana University Southeast, Texas Christian University, Clemson University, the Teaching & Learning Technology Group, the Appalachian College Association, Tuskegee Institute and the University of West Georgia.

THE SURVEY OF LIBRARY CAFÉS
ISBN: 1-57440-089-4   Price: $75.00   Publication Date: 2007

The Survey of Library Cafés presents data from more than 40 academic and public libraries about their cafés and other foodservice operations. The 60-page report gives extensive data and commentary on library café sales volume, best-selling products, impacts on library maintenance costs, reasons for starting a café, effects on library traffic, and many other issues regarding the decision to start and manage a library café.